THE BARE FACTS

THE BARE FACTS

39
Questions Your Parents Hope You Never Ask About
Sex

Josh McDowell
with Erin Davis

MOODY PUBLISHERS
CHICAGO

All Scripture quotations, unless otherwise indicated, are taken from the *Holy Bible, New International Version®*, NIV®. Copyright ©1973, 1978, 1984, 2011 by Biblica, Inc.™ Used by permission of Zondervan. All rights reserved worldwide. www.zondervan.com

Scripture quotations marked NASB are taken from the *New American Standard Bible®*, Copyright © 1960, 1962, 1963, 1968, 1971, 1972, 1973, 1975, 1977, 1995 by The Lockman Foundation. Used by permission. (www.Lockman.org)

Scripture quotations marked NLT are taken from the *Holy Bible, New Living Translation*, copyright © 1996, 2004. Used by permission of Tyndale House Publishers, Inc., Wheaton Illinois 60189, U.S.A. All rights reserved.

Scripture quotations marked ESV are taken from *The Holy Bible, English Standard Version*. Copyright © 2000, 2001 by Crossway Bibles, a division of Good News Publishers. Used by permission. All rights reserved.

Edited by Annette LaPlaca
Interior design: Rose DeBoer
Author Photo: Barbara Gannon

Cover design: Garborg Design Works
Cover image: iStock 000012512054

Library of Congress Cataloging-in-Publication Data

McDowell, Josh.
    The bare facts : 39 questions your parents hope you never ask about sex / Josh McDowell, with Erin Davis.
        p. cm.
    Includes bibliographical references.
    ISBN 978-0-8024-0255-4
    1. Sex—Religious aspects—Christianity. 2. Sex instruction for teenagers—Religious aspects—Christianity. 3. Christian teenagers—Sexual behavior. 4. Child rearing—Religious aspects—Christianity. I. Davis, Erin, 1980- II. Title.

BT708.M427 2011
241'.660835—dc22

2011013772

Also available as an EBook 978-0-8024-7838-2

All websites and phone numbers listed herein are accurate at the time of publication, but may change in the future or cease to exist. The listing of website references and resources does not imply publisher endorsement of the site's entire contents. Groups and organizations are listed for informational purposes, and listing does not imply publisher endorsement of their activities.

We hope you enjoy this book from Moody Publishers. Our goal is to provide high-quality, thought-provoking books and products that connect truth to your real needs and challenges. For more information on other books and products written and produced from a biblical perspective, go to www.moodypublishers.com or write to:

Moody Publishers
820 N. LaSalle Boulevard
Chicago, IL 60610

1 3 5 7 9 10 8 6 4 2

Printed in the United States of America

To
Sean, Stephanie, Scottie, Shauna, Kelly, Michael, Pippy, Katie, Jerry, Quinn, Beckett, Heather, David, Brenna, and Dottie.

My Family

CONTENTS

LET'S GET STARTED

RACHEL HAS BEEN RAISED in the church. She became a Christian at age ten. She's always gotten the impression from her parents and pastor that sex is a bad thing. She's now a freshman in college, and sex seems to be the only thing the girls in her dorm want to talk about. Even some of her friends from the Christian campus house talk about sex like it's no big deal. Rachel is starting to wonder, "When it comes to sex, what's all the fuss about?"

Nick has heard plenty about sex. It's a subject his youth pastor teaches on often (too often, in Nick's opinion). Nick is becoming a man, and his hormones seem to be screaming at him to have sex. He's decided if God didn't want him to have sex, He wouldn't have given him such strong sexual urges. Nick has decided it's unrealistic to wait until marriage.

Anna loves Jesus. Until recently she was active in her church and youth group and volunteered once a week at a local Christian preschool. In a moment of passion, Anna and her boyfriend had sex. Afterward, they seemed always to be fighting. They broke up last week. Now Anna is brokenhearted. She has dropped out of all activities at church, and she feels far away from God. She wants to be forgiven, but she's too ashamed to tell anyone, especially God, about her sin. She knows what the Bible says about forgiveness but she wonders if God could ever forgive her sexual sin.

If we asked Rachel, Nick, and Anna to tell us God's truth about sex, they'd be stumped. In a culture where sex is everywhere and purity has lost its meaning, young people, including those in the church, are left to face tremendous sexual temptation without an understanding of God's truth on the subject.

LOOKING FOR ANSWERS

The word "sex" receives 338 million Google searches a month. That's more than 4 billion searches a year, making it one of the top five most searched words ever.[1*] With teenagers making up the largest portion of Internet users, this trend reveals two things: 1) when it comes to sex, teenagers have questions, and 2) they are looking in the wrong place for answers.

The Bible isn't quiet on the subject of sex.

Christian researcher George Barna labeled today's teenagers the "Mosaic Generation" because of their tendency to take small pieces of information from many sources to create their own definition of truth.[2] This "whatever works" philosophy has infiltrated every dimension of this generation's decision making, especially their decisions about sex. Because Mosaics mix elements from many different beliefs, faith seems to have little or no impact on their approach to sex.

When researchers asked Mosaics about whether or not they cheat, view online porn, experiment with drugs and alcohol, or have sex, 53 percent of born-again teenagers admitted to at least one of those behaviors in the last three months, compared to 59 percent of unbelievers.[3]

LET'S TALK

Clearly, sex is a subject we need to talk about. Of the billions of people searching for answers about sex, many of them are asking one important question, "Why wait?" Maybe you are asking that exact question. Perhaps you want to know why you should save

---

* The most up-to-date notes are available online at www.josh.org.

sex until marriage and how you can say no in the meantime. Maybe you are a parent, pastor, youth leader, or teacher who feels ill-equipped to answer young people's questions about sex and to teach them why God's standard of purity is worth pursuing in a culture where anything goes.

You've come to the right place. I want you to know what God, medi-

No question is off-limits.

cine, and common sense say about sex. That's why I designed this book to offer honest, upfront, and intimate answers to the top questions students ask about sex, love, and relationships. No question is off-limits. After fifty years of speaking to more than 10 million young people, I've learned that knowledge, not ignorance, is the key that ultimately leads to a fulfilling marriage and family.

The culture's answers to your questions about sex will fall short, but that doesn't mean the answers can't be found. The Bible isn't quiet on the subject of sex. That's why we will use God's Word as our guide as we tackle your most burning questions about love and intimacy.

So pull up a chair. Grab a cup of coffee (I'll grab my Diet Coke), and settle in. Let's talk about sex.

Are abstinence and purity the same thing?

"Abstinence" has become the battle cry of the faith-based approach to sex—and secular programs have started to include abstinence as an "option" as part of a larger safer-sex agenda. But what is abstinence, exactly? And how does abstinence fit into God's plan for sex?

Abstinence simply means avoiding certain things. You can choose to abstain from specific foods or activities or events. When it comes to sexual education, proponents of the abstinence message want young people to say no to sex.

Surprisingly, Christians aren't the only ones pushing you to abstain. Members of the Harvard student group True Love Revolution urge their classmates to say no to sex based on philosophical, biological, and relational arguments.[4] The federal government pumps millions of dollars into abstinence-only programs every year.[5] Even Planned Parenthood promotes abstinence as a behavior that effectively prevents pregnancy and STDs.[6]

The world recognizes that there are strong reasons to abstain from sex, but God doesn't just call us to abstinence. He calls us to purity. So, then, what is purity?

That's a question I've been asking students for years. Sadly, I've never found anyone who can define purity. Can you believe that? Not one person. Not even pastors. Purity is one of the most beautiful concepts in the Bible, and no one seems to know what it means.

I want you to understand purity, because it's not what you think. Understanding purity will revolutionize how you think about sex.

Purity means—are you ready for this?—"to live according to original design."

In any area of your life, if you are living the way God designed you to live, you are pure. If you are not living the way God designed you to live, you are impure.

Purity is a commitment to live according to God's design.

Abstinence is a habit, or even a rule. Basically: Don't have sex!

Purity, though, is a virtue. It is not simply the choice to avoid sex. It is a commitment to live according to God's design. Purity means saying no to sex, but only so that you are able to experience sex within the loving marital relationship that God created.

2 Why are God and the Bible so negative about sex?

As our culture increasingly promotes sex without boundaries, God's view of sex seems more and more radical. Since the culture's message is progressively pro-sex, many people interpret God's message about sexuality to be anti-sex. *Nothing could be further from the truth.*

When it comes to God's view of sex, many people, including Christians, have mistaken God's serious approach to the subject to be negativity toward the subject. God does take sex very seriously. But the picture He gives us of sexuality is more intense, vibrant, and well . . . sexy . . . than the view taught by the culture. In fact, sticking to God's plan for sexuality leads to sex that is far more fulfilling than the sexual experiences supported by the world.

How do we know that God is pro-sex? Because of the dynamic picture of sex He paints in His Word.

In Proverbs, the writer speaks about a physical encounter that is satisfying and intoxicating (Proverbs 5:19). There's no anti-sex message here! But there's more.

The Song of Solomon is full of steamy descriptions of love scenes between a man and a woman. The book tells the story of two lovers totally immersed in satisfying each other. The love-making poetry is vivid and exciting, and God included it in His holy Word.

In the New Testament, the apostle Paul recommends sex between married couples often. The clear message is that God created sex for our enjoyment and His glory.

In fact, *there's not a single verse in the Bible that calls sex "sinful" or "dirty."* The verses that are often quoted to paint sex in a negative light aren't about sex at all. They are about the misuse of sex outside of God's design.

God desires us to experience sex at its best.

God designed sex as a gift to be shared between a husband and wife. As the original designer, God created this sexual experience to be the most exciting and satisfying. God's message about sex isn't, "Don't do it because it is sinful or wrong." His message is, "Wait—because sex according to this design is so wonderful that it's worth protecting."

For Christians struggling to understand God's plan for sex, the real question isn't, "Why is God so negative about sex?" but rather, "Is God really good?"

God's plan for sex is clearly outlined in the Scriptures. He wants us to enjoy sex, but He asks us to wait until we are married. The world teaches that God's request to wait is proof that He wants to deny what's good for us. But nothing could be further from the truth.

Jeremiah 29:11 makes this promise, "'For I know the plans I have for you,' declares the Lord, 'plans to prosper you and not to harm you, plans to give you hope and a future.'"

Psalm 31:19 says, "How abundant are the good things that you have stored up for those who fear you, that you bestow in the sight of all, on those who take refuge in you."

God's desire is to give us good things. The boundaries He places on sex are for our protection, not our deprivation. The world may see limits on sexuality as negative, but the opposite is true. God isn't against sex. He's so for it that He wants every man and woman to experience sex according to His original design.

If we choose to believe God when He promises He has good things in store for us, we can freely embrace His plan for sex knowing He desires us to experience sex at its best.

3 Why did God even create sex?

The Bible gives us three specific reasons for sex. The first one might seem familiar, but keep reading. God's plan for sex isn't as boring as you might think.

#1: PROCREATION

You probably already know about the first reason for why God created sex. It's called procreation—that is, making babies.

In Genesis 1:28 God revealed this purpose for sex to Adam and Eve when He said, "Be fruitful and increase in number; fill the earth and subdue it."

God has given us a very God-like ability to create life through the act of sex. The beginning of this verse tells us that God intended the results of sex to be a blessing. When children are born out of a lifelong commitment between a man and a woman, the blessing is tremendous!

Of course it is possible to make babies outside of marriage. But creating life is one of the most amazing things you will ever do. It deserves to be celebrated without the shame and distractions of bad timing, within the bounds of a God-honoring marriage.

#2: UNITY

As humans, we are hardwired with a deep desire for intimacy. We long to connect with other humans and with God. God created this desire within us. Part of His design for sex includes meeting that need for personal connection.

Sex is scientifically proven to create a bond between two people, but

God wants sex to be fun!

the deepest levels of connection and intimacy can only be achieved by pursuing God's plan for sex.

Genesis 2:24 says, "This explains why a man leaves his father and mother and is joined to his wife, and the two are united into one" (NLT).

This passage talks about the bond between a husband and wife becoming so strong that they become "united into one." In other words, they are so joined together that you cannot pull them apart.

The writer of Genesis knew intuitively what science has recently confirmed. Researchers have discovered a hormone called oxytocin, or the "cuddle hormone."[7] Oxytocin is a chemical your brain releases during sex and the activity leading up to it. When this chemical is released, it produces feelings of caring, trust, and deep affection. The same chemical is released when a mom breastfeeds her new baby. The purpose is to create a deep human bond or attachment.

Every time you have sex with another person, your body has a chemical reaction that tells it to "cleave." God created the means to meet your desire for intimacy at a biological level—but there's a catch. Research has proven that God's design for intimacy is at its best between a husband and wife with no other sexual partners.

A University of Chicago survey found that monogamous married couples register the highest levels of sexual satisfaction. According to the survey, 87 percent of all monogamous married couples report that they are "extremely" or "very" physically satisfied by their sexual relationship and 85 percent that they are "extremely" or "very" emotionally satisfied.[8] In other words, the oxytocin is flowing freely in the brains of many married couples! Remarkably, those who are least satisfied (both physically and emotionally) are those singles and marrieds who have multiple partners.

A review of longitudinal research by the National Center for Health Statistics and the University of Maryland found that women who save sex for marriage face a considerably lower risk of divorce than those who are sexually active prior to marriage.[9] When we follow God's design for sex, we are able to form a bond with our spouse that is difficult to break (remember how Genesis said that was when "two are united into one"?).

When we wait until marriage to have sex, we establish a level of intimacy that is unequaled.

#3: RECREATION

We've already established that God is pro-sex and that He desires good things for you. Here's proof: One of the reasons God created sex was for our enjoyment. That's right! *God wants sex to be fun!*

We see this clearly in Proverbs 5:18–19: "Let your wife be a fountain of blessing for you. Rejoice in the wife of your youth. She is a loving deer, a graceful doe. Let her breasts satisfy you always. May you always be captivated by her love" (NLT). Steamy, right? This passage talks about a husband being satisfied by his wife's body. The original text reads more like, "May you be intoxicated by her sex." God intended sex to be exciting and enjoyable.

It is true that sex outside of marriage can be fun, but it cannot reach the level of enjoyment and pleasure that we find when we stick to God's plan for sex.

God created sex for our benefit and His glory.

Once again, research proves that God's design leads to the best sex. Most major studies show a strong correlation between monogamous marriage and sexual satisfaction. Those same studies indicate that women who engage in early sexual activity and those who have had multiple partners are less satisfied with their sex lives than women who entered marriage with little or no sexual experience. *USA Today* called this research "the revenge of the church ladies."[10]

The world teaches that sex without limits is the most fun, but research has proven what God's Word already teaches. God wants us to enjoy sex. When we stick to His plan for our sexuality we find a level of enjoyment and pleasure that cannot be matched.

So why did God create sex? Clearly, He did it for our benefit and His glory. When sex is enjoyed according to God's plan, the result is amazing! When we move outside of the boundaries God has established for our sex lives, pleasure is weakened, intimacy is cheapened, and the blessings God intended as the results of our sexual encounters can spoil.

4 How do you define "love"?

Most young people, both girls and boys, claim that being in love is the reason for beginning sexual activity. Clearly, love is a powerful motivator of behavior, and yet most of us struggle to define what love is.

Love is perhaps the most talked about, written about, and sung about subject in all of history. From movies, to music, to poetry, everyone seems to offer a different definition for love.

- "Love means never having to say you're sorry"—from the movie *Love Story*.
- "Love is a verb"—lyrics by dc Talk.
- "Love is passion, obsession, someone you can't live without" —from the movie *Meet Joe Black*.
- "Love is friendship on fire"—from the movie *The Perfect Man*.

Most definitions of love make for catchy song lyrics or romantic movie scripts, but do they hold up in the real world? When applied to our relationships and sexual experiences, do we even know what love really is?

Love is one of the most intricate and powerful concepts in the world, and yet I have found that very few people seem to understand it. Defining love is a critical step toward understanding God's purpose and design for sex. After all, if you cannot define love, how do you know if you *are* in love? If you cannot define love, how can you know if you are *being* loved? If you cannot define love, how do you know if you *have* a loving, intimate relationship? If you cannot define love, how can you *express* love through sex? You can't.

In order to fully understand what love is, let's take a look at what it isn't.

LOVE ISN'T A FEELING.

When you were little, your mother could command you to eat your vegetables (that's an action), but she couldn't command you to like them (that's a feeling). When I ask people to define love for me, most of them tell me it's a feeling. But love cannot be a feeling because you cannot command an emotion. You can only command an action or a decision.

Who can command us to love? God can and does!

John 13:34 says, "A new command I give you: Love one another. As I have loved you, so you must love one another."

Ephesians 5:25 states, "Husbands, love your wives, just as Christ loved the church and gave himself up for her."

Clearly, love is more than a feeling. It is a series of choices. When we choose to love, our emotions can be transformed, but love is expressed by acts of the will.

LOVE ISN'T SEX.

Our culture teaches that "love" and "sex" are interchangeable words, and that sex is a measuring tool to gauge whether or not you are in love. It further teaches that sex is a necessary component for a loving relationship. But God's Word gives us a definition of love that has nothing to do with sex. Unmistakably, sex and love are *not* the same.

What is it about sex and love that makes them so easy to mix up? Remember in the answer to question 3,

Sex and love are *not* the same.

I stated that during sexual activity the brain releases oxytocin, a "cuddle hormone" that produces feelings of caring, trust, and deep affection. That "feeling," combined with pop-culture's attempt to sell sex and love as one package, can lead many to think that sex equals love. Since we already know that love isn't a feeling and we can determine that the world's definition of love is inconsistent at best, undeniably sex is *not* love.

Since God designed sex to bond us to each other, when we choose to engage in sex outside of marriage it turns relationships upside down and confuses emotions to the point where a person can misinterpret sex for love. When we follow God's plan, the love between a man and woman is already established *before* sex enters the equation.

Choosing to gratify your immediate needs now by ignoring God's plan for sex is not an expression of love. True love will wait until marriage in order to protect you and your partner from the potential dangers of extramarital sex, and it will provide for a future where sex is at its best.

GOD'S DEFINITION OF LOVE

God's Word offers a clear definition of love. Stick with me here as we trace the word "love" through several passages to find a definition with the power to radically impact how we live.

In Matthew 22:39 Jesus says, "Love your neighbor as yourself."

How are we to love others? The way we love ourselves. This passage isn't talking about a narcissistic self-love. We love ourselves by consistently making sure our needs are met. Thus, true love will desire to meet the needs of the one being loved.

Ephesians 5:28–29 (ESV) offers another clue toward God's definition of love. It says, "In the same way husbands should love their wives as their own bodies. He who loves his wife loves himself. For no one ever hated his own flesh, but nourishes and cherishes it, just as Christ does the church."

How do we specifically love ourselves? By nourishing and cherishing. If I love myself in a biblical way, then I will nourish myself to maturity physically, spiritually, mentally, and relationally.

If I truly love myself, I will cherish or protect myself from anything that will hinder that nurturing process.

God's Word provides the simplest definition of love—to protect and provide. True love always, without exception, seeks the best interest of the loved one. Its motivation is always to "protect and provide."

How does sex fit into God's definition of love? When sex is confined to marriage, it is a beautiful way to provide for the physical and emotional needs of your partner. But outside of marriage, sex opens you and your partner up to harm. When you choose to engage in sex outside of marriage, you fail to

True love's motivation is always to "protect and provide."

protect your partner (and yourself) from the potential for devastating consequences like unplanned pregnancy, STDs, guilt, heartbreak, and hindered goals.

When we operate outside of God's design, the lines between love and sex get blurred. Don't confuse warm feelings for love. And don't buy the lie that sex is the best way to express your love for someone you care for. God designed sex for marriage for our own protection. When the happiness, security, spiritual growth, and health of another person is as important to you as your own—so much so that you desire to protect him or her from the potential harm that sex outside of marriage can bring—then you know that you've found love.

5 What does the Bible mean when it says, "God is love"?

Our ability to fully understand and embrace God's plan for sex hinges entirely on our understanding of who He is.

First John 4:16 describes God this way: "And so we know and rely on the love God has for us. *God is love.* Whoever lives in love lives in God, and God in them" (emphasis added).

First John 4:8 tells us: "Whoever does not love does not know God, because *God is love*" (emphasis added).

The statement "God is love" doesn't mean that God is a vague, warm, fuzzy feeling. Remember, we've already established that love isn't a feeling. So, what does God's love really look like?

In John 15:12–13 Jesus said, "My command is this: Love each other as I have loved you. Greater love has no one than this: to lay down one's life for one's friends."

God is the ultimate example of what love is and how love behaves. Jesus demonstrated this by living a life of love and compassion here on earth. His death on the cross gives us a picture of God's love in action. His dramatic love for us is the standard by which He asks us to love others.

God doesn't just say that He loves us. He doesn't send us a cosmic Valentine from heaven and fail to put His love into action. He demonstrates His love for us over and over and over.

You might say, "Wait a minute! If God loves me so much why does He want to deprive me of good things, like sex?"

Let's go back to the definition of love we discussed in the answer to the last question. Love means to protect and provide. God's commands aren't meant to deprive or restrict us, rather they are meant to provide for our good and protect our future.

There are several commandments throughout the Bible where God asks us to say no to specific choices and behaviors. Though these commandments may appear negative at first glance, they are really a profound expression of God's love. In fact, every time God says, "Thou shalt not," He is proving His love by protecting and providing for us.

Deuteronomy 10:13 says, "Observe the Lord's commands and decrees that I am giving you today for *your own good*" (emphasis added).

God's commands are meant to provide for our good and protect our future.

■ ■ ■ ■ ■ ■ ■ ■ ■ ■

Why does God give us commandments? For our own good! Even when God's ways feel frustrating or restrictive, we can know that He loves us and His directives were designed to protect and provide for us.

God's commandments regarding sex are the perfect example of this principle.

In 1 Corinthians 6:18 we read, "Flee from sexual immorality. All other sins a person commits are outside the body, but whoever sins sexually, sins against their own body."

God clearly asks us to avoid sexual immorality. Why? He gives us the answer in the same passage in which He asks us to wait.

"Whoever sins sexually, sins against their own body." Having sex outside of God's design will literally affect your body physically. When you operate outside of God's plan for sex, your body can suffer serious consequences. Here's some evidence:

- Approximately one in four sexually active young adults ages 15 to 24 contracts an STD each year.[11]
- In 2004, the CDC estimated that more than 18,000 young people, ages thirteen to twenty-four, were living with

HIV/AIDS (in the thirty-five areas with confidential name-based HIV reporting); almost 5,000 were diagnosed in 2004 alone, representing 3 percent of all people diagnosed that year.[12]

- In 2009, a total of 409,840 infants were born to fifteen- to nineteen-year-olds.[13] Well over half of those pregnancies were unintended.[14]

Almost all of these health risks are eliminated when two people wait for marriage to experience sex. Even the challenges associated with unplanned pregnancy are lessened when a baby is conceived in the context of a loving, committed marital relationship.

Clearly, God doesn't ask us to wait for sex in order to spoil our fun or restrict us unnecessarily. His commandments regarding sex are evidence of His love for us as He seeks to protect and provide for our good.

Because "God is love" He seeks our well-being at every turn. When we understand the Bible in this light, we are free to embrace His commandments knowing they are written by a loving God, who knows what's best for us.

6 What is a person's most powerful sex organ?

Your most powerful sex organ isn't covered by your swimsuit. The key to maximum sex isn't found between your legs. It's between your ears. When it comes to sex, your brain is where the real magic happens.

Here's a crash course in the science of your brain. Though weighing only three pounds, your brain contains 10 billion neurons,

100 billion support cells, and 100 trillion connectors that connect those cells and neurons.[15] Every second one million new connectors are created.[16] Your brain is the most intricate mass in the universe.

Within that intricate mass of cells and connectors, the most exciting elements of sex are experienced. You've heard the word "orgasm," right? It describes an intense feeling of pleasure during sex. Researchers have discovered that during an orgasm the brain lights up after receiving a massive dose of feel-good

Almost two-thirds of sexually active students wish they had waited.
■ ■ ■ ■ ■ ■ ■ ■ ■ ■

chemicals. During sex, the brain sends messages through the body commanding physical function. Without nerves sending impulses back to the spinal cord, an orgasm wouldn't be possible. When it comes to responding to sexual experiences, clearly the brain is calling the shots.

But not all brains are equipped for maximum sex. Remember those hundred trillion connectors? When you are born, those connectors are bare. Starting in your teenage years, insulation called "myelin" forms around those connectors. Myelin continues to be formed well into your twenties. This "myelin shaft" acts just like insulation on an electrical cord. It allows the electrical impulses being sent by your brain to travel down the nerve faster and more efficiently.[17] Some of the nerves that become coated during adolescence connect areas of the brain that regulate emotion, judgment, and impulse control. In other words, your brain doesn't become hardwired to make fast, wise choices about sex until you are in your twenties.

Neuroscientists have discovered that adolescent brains are still maturing in other areas as well. One of the last parts of our brains to mature is the system in charge of making sound judgments and calming unruly emotions. It's called "the prefrontal cortex."[18]

When we are born, we operate out of the limbic system, which is found in the back, inner part of our brain. The limbic system is basically where we find raw emotion. When we function from our limbic system, we are unable to make choices based on right or wrong; we can decide only based on how we feel.

Later in life, our control center for decision making moves from the limbic system to the prefrontal cortex—which is found in the front of the brain. From the prefrontal cortex we are able to make moral choices. The limbic system deals with urges and appetites. Only the prefrontal cortex is able to make consistent choices based on future consequences. Think of it this way: if the limbic system is a hungry lion, the prefrontal cortex is a well-trained lion tamer. The lion just wants to eat and doesn't think about what may happen if he homes in on the wrong target for lunch. The lion tamer uses rewards and consequences to tame the lion's animalistic appetites.

Scientifically speaking, young people are lions. During the teen years, the prefrontal cortex is practically asleep at the wheel and the limbic system is in hyperdrive. In fact, the switch from functioning from the limbic system to functioning from the prefrontal cortex isn't normally completed until the midtwenties. Biologically speaking, the average teenager's prefrontal cortex isn't quite ready to take on the role of brain CEO or "boss,"[19] but young people in this stage of development are making decisions about sex that will have consequences for the rest of their lives.

A recent survey by the *Journal of Youth and Adolescence* found that more than 60 percent of seventeen- to eighteen-year-olds have had sex.[20] Yet their brains are not fully equipped to make choices based on future consequences. Maybe that's why almost two-thirds of sexually active students wish they had waited.[21]

Teenagers may be physically ready for sex, but their most powerful sex organ, the brain, isn't equipped for maximum sex until much later.

Let's go back to the purposes of sex from question 3. Remember that God created sex for our enjoyment and to bond us to another person.

Your most powerful sex organ isn't covered by your swimsuit.

These two purposes of sex aren't biological but mental. By God's design, the best rewards for sex happen in your mind.

In other words, *no one has yet developed a condom for the mind.* Only God is able to protect our most powerful sex organ until we have that relationship in which we are able to fully enjoy the mental, emotional, and physical pleasure that sex provides.

Here's some good advice from God's Word: "Do not be conformed to this world, but be transformed by the renewal of your mind, that by testing you may discern what is the will of God, what is good and acceptable and perfect" (Romans 12:2 ESV).

7 Can sex affect my brain?

We've established that your brain is your most powerful sex organ. The way your brain responds to sex long term is dramatically influenced by the choices you make about sexual activity.

Remember that 1 Corinthians 6:18 warns us to avoid sex outside of God's design because doing so is a sin against our own body. Scientists now back up Paul's warning by establishing that when you engage in sex outside of marriage, there are physical consequences in your brain.

Let's follow the data on the science of sex to discover how sex changes your most powerful sex organ.

BONDING HAPPENS IN THE BRAIN.

Remember the "cuddle hormone" oxytocin? It is the bonding hormone released during sexual activity that creates feelings of caring, trust, and deep affection. The unity factor that we all crave and that God designed sex to satisfy is literally built into our minds.

Female brains receive especially high doses of oxytocin whenever there is touching and hugging. Vasopressin is a hormone that does the same thing in the male brain.[22]

In the context of a loving, committed relationship, the brain releases increasing levels of oxytocin and vasopressin to keep the bond secure. God has designed our bodies to respond physically to long-term intimacy, and that response takes place in the brain. When we continually change partners, oxytocin levels decrease and the brain's oxytocin release function doesn't work as it's supposed to. Promiscuous sexual activity wears down vasopressin production in the male brain, causing men to become desensitized to the risk of short-term relationships.[23] Short-term, noncommital sex can literally change your brain at a chemical level.

Oxytocin and vasopressin aren't the only sexual responses generated in the brain. Sex also triggers a "feel good" chemical called dopamine. Dopamine is released anytime we do something exciting or rewarding. If oxytocin is the chemical that tells us we're in love, dopamine says, "I've got to have more of that!" Researchers have pinpointed high levels of dopamine in the brains of couples newly in love.[24] Dopamine stimulates desire by triggering an intense rush of pleasure in the brain.

It's important to understand that dopamine is value-neutral.[25] It cannot tell the difference between constructive and destructive behaviors or between good and bad relationships. In many ways, dopamine works like a drug. Our brains need increasing doses in order to achieve the same level of pleasure. Sex outside of marriage causes an increasing craving for dopamine that has serious consequences on our relationships. If the relationship ends, it affects the release of oxytocin, and more and more sexual contact is required to get the same dopamine rush. Every time you move to a new relationship, you have to have a little more sexual contact in order to satisfy your brain's craving for dopamine, and the bonding effect starts to break down. Also, because dopamine triggers intense feelings of pleasure, sexually active couples often substitute that feeling of excitement for feelings of affection. Their relationships quickly deteriorate as they start chasing the dopamine high instead of chasing true intimacy. Sex addiction is another potential pitfall that can happen in the brain. It is possible to become addicted to the brain/chemical response that happens during sex, and then the struggle to rein in sexual appetite grows more and more difficult.

When sex is reserved for marriage, our brains still receive doses of the neurochemicals that make sex so exciting, and our brains are then able to process those chemicals in a way that promotes healthy relationships and responses.

SEX AFFECTS YOUR MEMORY.

There is even compelling evidence that your experiences affect your brain. Any time you are in an emotional situation with your five senses involved, your body releases a chemical called norepinephrine. Norepinephrine is the "memory chemical." When you experience a highly emotional and sensory event, norepinephrine is released in your brain. It takes that experience and "paper-clips" it to your brain for recall. Since sexual encounters are highly emotional and sensory, your brain responds with a dose of this memory chemical and attaches each experience to your mind.

When you get married, you will bring those paper-clipped experiences into the relationship with you. You might say, "When I meet the person I want to be with forever, I won't even remember the other people I've been with." It simply doesn't work that way. Your sexual encounters are imprinted into your brain. It happens at a biological level. You won't be able to shake the memory of your other sex partners because they have changed the landscape of your brain.

Hebrews 13:4 tells us, "Marriage should be honored by all, and the marriage bed kept pure." This verse is better translated as "Let sexual intercourse be pure." One definition of purity is "containing no foreign element."[26] When we don't wait until marriage for sex, mentally we are bringing our other sexual partners into the marriage bed because they are permanently imprinted on our minds and affect how we respond at a chemical level.

You won't be able to shake the memory of your other sex partners.

After a speaking engagement, a friend of mine who is a pastor asked to take me to the airport. The previous night I had spoken on sex, and as we got in the car and started traveling, my friend was very quiet. Finally he said, "Josh, I need your help. I've been married for almost two decades to a beautiful woman, but I've never, ever been in bed alone with her."

"What do you mean?" I asked.

"When I was in high school I wasn't a believer, and I played around sexually—a lot," he confessed. "It carried right over into the university. In college I trusted Christ as Savior and Lord, but one area I didn't change was my sex life. Then I met my wife during my junior year. Up until then, I never knew there was any woman as beautiful as she was. We fell in love, and we got married."

He went on to describe the impact his sexual sin had on his marriage. "Starting on my wedding night, all the flashbacks, the reruns in the theater of my mind, kept coming back from all those other girls." This man had the ghosts of relationships past physically paper-clipped into his brain. The results he reported were terribly destructive.

The clear verdict is that each of us changes the very structure of our brains with the choices we make and the behavior we are involved in.

8 Hasn't modern medicine eliminated STDs and infections?

Many students seem to think that medicine has eliminated the risk of sexually transmitted diseases (STDs) and can provide an easy cure in the rare case of infection. Unfortunately, their information is dead wrong.

In the 1960s doctors treated two main STDs—syphilis and gonorrhea. Both diseases could be cured with a shot. Today, doctors recognize twenty-five major STDs,[27] nineteen of which have *no cure*.[28]

In the 1960s one out of every sixty sexually active teens got an STD. By the 1970s that number jumped to one out of every forty-seven.[29] Today one in four sexually active teenagers is infected.[30]

Despite efforts to cure STDs and to curb their spread, the variety and scope of STD infection is increasing, not decreasing. Right now there are 70 million Americans living with an STD.[31] Approximately 65 million of those cases are incurable.[32] Worldwide, nearly 330 million people are infected with STDs each year.[33]

Young people are especially vulnerable to infection. Within two years of their first sexual encounter, half of teenage girls are infected with at least one of three common STDs. The Centers for Disease Control (CDC) estimate that 19 million new STD infections appear each year in America. Almost half of those occur among fifteen- to twenty-year-olds.[34]

Today, one in four sexually active teenagers is infected.

It is nearly impossible to play around sexually and beat the odds. If you choose to engage in premarital sex, your chance of infection is at least one in four.[35] As you add sexual partners, the numbers start to compound.

You may look at those numbers and think, "If only one in four sexually active teenagers has an STD, that means I have a chance of avoiding infection. Besides, they've got medicine for these diseases, right?" Wrong! Most STDs are incurable because they are viruses. All viruses are incurable, from STDs to the common cold. There are treatments for some STDs, but many of them are long, painful treatments necessary after only one moment of pleasure. Even some treatable STDs are beginning to show resistance to treatment.

Each year, identifying and treating STDs comes with a $16 billion price tag to the health care system.[36] Medical researchers are constantly working to combat that huge number of STDs with new treatments.

One recent development is a vaccine for the most common STD: HPV, or human papillomavirus. Many championed the vaccine as a major step in the fight against STDs, but in reality, the vaccine offers little protection from the actual risk. For starters, the HPV vaccine is only for women. So far there is no vaccine for men. The vaccine is only 70 percent effective. It must be taken when you are young, and it will not work if you are a woman who is already infected. The vaccine doesn't deal with all of the HPV viruses that cause cancer. The duration of the immunity following vaccination is unknown. Since this is a new drug, it could take years to find out how long immunity will last for the 70 percent of women affected by the vaccine.[37] Again, the odds of protection are not high.

Beyond illness, the consequences of STD infection are devastating. Approximately 100,000 women in the U.S. between the ages of fifteen and twenty-five will never be able to have children because of an STD.[38] The CDC estimates that almost 8,000 men get HPV-related cancer annually.[39] More than 17,000 Americans die from AIDS each year.[40]

If you are going to have sex outside of God's protective boundaries, the odds of escaping an STD are against you. Science has proven that.

The medical community recognizes these odds. So does the government. In fact, the government recently allocated $400 million to the CDC for the screening and prevention of STDs.[41] Yet, the incidence of STD infection is growing. Simply put, we cannot expect the government or the medical community to protect us from the consequences of a choice God clearly warns us against.

Doctors recognize twenty-five major STDs, nineteen of which have *no cure*.

Remember that God's guidelines for sex were created to protect and provide for you. What are the odds of contracting a sexually transmitted disease in a pure marriage relationship? *Zero*. Now those are odds you can live with.

9 What is the most common STD?

Most of us, teenagers and adults, are shockingly uninformed on the subject of STDs. Very few people have even heard of the most common STD or are aware that it is incurable.[42] What is it? Human papillomavirus (HPV).

HPV is a sexually transmitted viral infection. It is easily transmitted and is not usually contained by condoms. Perhaps that's why the CDC recognizes HPV as the number one STD in the U.S. and worldwide.[43]

One source reports that almost 6 million Americans are infected each year with HPV.[44] To help you grasp how many people that includes, 6 million is almost twice the size of the population of Los Angeles, California. Break that number down and 458,333 people are infected each month. That's approximately the size of the population of New Orleans. More than 100,000 people are infected with HPV each week. That's equal to the size of the entire population of Green Bay, Wisconsin. More than 15,000 sexually active individuals are infected daily, 627 are infected each hour, and 19 people are infected every single minute. Right now, 20 million Americans are infected with HPV.[45] That's approximately the same number of people living on the entire continent of Australia!

A closer look at the data about HPV reveals more shocking numbers.

- 80 percent of all women will have HPV by the time they are fifty.[46]
- 70 percent of sexually involved men get HPV.[47]

- 50 percent of sexually active individuals are now, or previously have been infected with HPV.[48]
- 80 million Americans between the ages of fifteen and forty-nine have been infected by genital HPV at some point in their lives.[49]
- Twenty- to twenty-four-year-olds have the highest rate of infection of HPV: 26.8 percent of men and women in this age bracket are infected.[50]

Keep in mind that countless numbers of HPV cases are never reported due to shame, embarrassment, denial, or lack of symptoms.

Because HPV is a virus, there is no cure. Because the virus grows on moist skin, it is passed easily. Experts estimate that the transmission rate with each act of sexual intercourse with an HPV infected partner is 50 percent. Up to 90 percent of sexual partners of infected people also become infected.[51]

Part of the high transmission rate is due to the fact that the virus often fails to show any symptoms for long periods of time. HPV can "hide" in the body for years without being detected.[52]

The greatest risk associated with HPV is cancer. Up to 70 percent of females infected with HPV will later develop precancerous changes of the cervix.[53] HPV has been linked to

Right now, 20 million Americans are infected with HPV.

more than 90 percent of all invasive cervical cancers, which is the number two cause of cancer deaths among women after breast cancer.[54] HPV-induced cervical cancer occurs in 13,000 American women each year. Approximately 5,000 die from the disease.[55]

In the past five years, HPV has killed more women than HIV and AIDS.[56] And yet HPV is a disease that is rarely talked about. UCLA medical school found that in more than 90 percent of all cervical and vulvar cancer (it is epidemic) in women there was the presence of HPV.[57] This is why the CDC says this cancer is sexually transmitted.[58]

Can men get HPV? You bet! Eighty percent of women will become infected with HPV by the time they turn fifty, but that doesn't mean that HPV is a women's disease. An alarming new international study funded by the US National Cancer Institute found that 50 percent of eighteen- to seventy-year-old men (whether they have been sexually involved or not) in Brazil, Mexico, and the U.S. are infected with the disease.[59]

Very few young people even realize that HPV is a risk associated with sexual activity. Even fewer understand the overwhelming odds of contracting HPV, and very few people grasp that HPV can kill.

When it comes to HPV, the medical community has released big numbers that represent a big problem. God sees the scope of this disease, but He is most interested in a much smaller number. When God gave us parameters for sex, He had one person in mind—you. He asks you to make one choice: to wait for one person, your spouse. Clearly, the stats on HPV indicate that His motivation was to protect one body and one future—yours.

10 Do women get more STDs than men?

Guys are more sexually active than girls, and yet girls are more likely to get an STD.[60] For example, one study showed that 21 percent of women are infected with genital herpes (HSV) compared with only 11.5 percent of men.[61] Of the twenty-five principal STDs, most of them primarily damage women.

Why are women more at risk? It boils down to biology. Most STDs are viruses. They grow and multiply in a warm, moist environment without oxygen, such as the female genitals, not a man's penis. Any virus transferred to the male penis cannot survive once exposed to oxygen. The end result is that women are much easier to infect and damage. It is a devastating reality.

Guys are more sexually active than girls, and yet girls are twice as likely to get an STD.

Here are a few of the sobering facts about women and STDs:

- 80–90 percent of women infected with chlamydia have no symptoms.[62]
- The vague symptoms associated with pelvic inflammatory disease (PID) cause 85 percent of women to delay seeking medical care, greatly increasing their risk for infertility.[63]
- Syphilis rates among women increased 36 percent from 2007 to 2008.[64]
- Cervical cancer rates are increasing among young women,[65] which may reflect an increased exposure to STDs, including HPV.
- The number of women with HIV will soon outnumber men with HIV.[66]
- Women who are infected with an STD while pregnant can have early onset of labor, premature rupture of membranes, or uterine infection before and after delivery.[67]
- It is estimated that 30–40 percent of preterm births and infant deaths are due to STDs.[68]

The most common consequence of STD infection for women is infertility. STDs cause infertility in women by causing irreversible

scarring in the fallopian tubes and uterine lining. Men can be exposed to the same STDs without risking infertility because their reproductive organs are not scarred. For other women, the end result
of infection is cervical cancer. Obviously, men are immune from
cervical cancer because they do not have a cervix.

Clearly, when God's boundaries for sex are ignored, people—
especially women—pay a huge price.

11 Is it true that young people get more STDs than any other age group?

One of the hallmarks of adolescence is a sense
of invincibility rooted in the notion that bad
things only happen to "someone else." When it comes to teenagers
and sex, the reality couldn't be any more startling.

Our culture defines young people as those between the ages of
twelve and twenty-five. In the U.S. young people make up 17 percent of the population. And yet two-thirds of all STDs occur in
people under age twenty-five.[69]

A total of 19 million STDs are contracted each year in the U.S.[70]
Three million STDs are contracted by thirteen- to nineteen-year-
olds in the U.S. each year.[71] More than 9 million STDs are contracted by Americans ages fifteen to twenty-four each year.[72] This
means that roughly two-thirds of STDs are contracted by only 17
percent of the U.S. population.[73]

Within two years of having sex for the first time, 50 percent of
teenagers will get infected with an STD.[74] Approximately 25 percent of sexually active teens get an STD each year.[75] That's not a

one-in-four shot of contracting an STD while in high school. That's a one-in-four shot of being infected *every year* of high school. Of teens having sex, one out of every three will graduate from high school with a diploma and a sexually transmitted disease.

Don't gloss over these numbers. Take a minute to allow these sobering facts about young people and STDs to soak in.

- In 2006, adolescents and young adults ages thirteen to twenty-nine accounted for the greatest increase of new HIV infections (34 percent)—more than any other group.[76]
- Three out of five Americans living with HIV were infected as teenagers.[77]
- Although youth are at higher risk for acquiring STDs, only one-third of sexually active teens (ages fifteen to seventeen) and one-half of sexually active young adults (ages eighteen to twenty-four) have been tested for an STD.[78]
- Teens are up to ten times more susceptible to pelvic inflammatory disease (PID) than adults,[79] the end result of which is infertility for many young women.
- In 2002, 50 percent of the cases of chlamydia reported by the CDC were in teenagers.[80]
- In 2002, gonorrhea was the most commonly reported infectious disease among people fifteen to twenty-four.[81]
- Almost 25,000 fifteen- to -twenty-four-year-olds get an STD every single day. That breaks down to 1,039 every hour.[82]

Why are teens more susceptible to sexually transmitted disease? The two simple answers are: *biology* and *behavior.*

The biological reasons for young people's high susceptibility to STDs relate specifically to females. Within her cervical lining, a young girl has high amounts of cells called "columnar cells."

These cells are exposed throughout the entire cervix lining.[83] As she grows older, those columnar cells are layered over with squamous epithelium cells. These cells start to form layers and eventually completely encompass the columnar cells.[84] But this process isn't completed until a woman is in her midtwenties.

Of teens having sex, one out of every three will graduate from high school with a diploma and a sexually transmitted disease.

What's the difference between the two types of cells? Columnar cells are extremely receptive. Think of them as wet sponges. Any disease that comes into contact with these cells will almost certainly stick, just as dirt or sand would stick to a wet sponge. In fact, columnar cells are more than 80 percent more receptive to infections than the squamous epithelium cells found in the cervix of a woman who is older than twenty-five.[85]

By her midtwenties a woman's cervix starts to harden and reject the viruses it comes into contact with. If columnar cells are like a wet sponge, squamous epithelium cells are more like a dry sponge that has never been used. Because it is hard and compacted, sand and dirt would be more likely to bounce off the dry sponge.

But we're not talking about dirt here. We are talking about viruses that pose serious risk to the health of young women and their male sexual partners. For example, a fifteen-year-old girl has a one-in-eight chance of developing pelvic inflammatory disease simply by having sex, whereas a twenty-four-year-old woman has only a one-in-eighty chance in the same situation.[86] Another difference in the cervix lining of a young woman is that the columnar cells pass the virus right into the bloodstream, and in an older woman it is much more difficult for the virus to get into the blood. In general, a teenager is 80 percent more likely to get an STD than somebody older than twenty-five.[87]

Did you notice that the changes in a woman's cervix happen at the exact same stage in life that the brain switches from the limbic system (raw emotion) to the prefrontal cortex (moral decision making)? Clearly, God has equipped us for maximum sex when we wait for His timing.

Biology isn't the only factor putting young people at risk for exposure to STDs. Many young people are making behavioral choices that make them prime targets for infection. The CDC reports that teenagers are most likely to choose sexual partners older than themselves. Sexually active teenagers are also very likely to have sex with multiple partners, compounding their risk of infection. One study found that 75 percent of teenagers who initiate intercourse before age eighteen have two or more partners, and 45 percent have four or more partners.[88]

God has equipped us for maximum sex when we wait for His timing.

The number of young people infected with STDs continues to spiral upward at an alarming rate. The individual cost of this trend is clearly too high.

What does God say on the subject? Check out 1 Timothy 4:12: "Don't let anyone think less of you because you are young. Be an example to all believers in what you say, in the way you live, in your love, your faith, and your purity" (NLT).

Who will raise the bar when it comes to young people and sex? Who will be an example in the way that they live and their standards of purity? Who will decide that the risks are too high and that God's design is best? Will you?

12 Isn't it safe sex if we use a condom?

Your generation has been given the message that condoms equal safe sex and that safe sex frees you to enjoy sex without risks. You have been lied to.

Several years ago, propagators of the safe sex message made a subtle change to their message. Now instead of promoting "safe sex," condom supporters urge young people to have "safer sex." Why the switch? Because a look at the facts shows that condoms aren't safe. You can use a condom and still get STDs. You can use a condom and still get pregnant. And no condom will ever protect you from the mental and emotional pitfalls of sex outside of God's design.

CONDOMS AND STDS

Scientifically, it is impossible to "wear a condom and have safe sex." The best that could be said would be, "Wear a condom and experience less dangerous sex" (from a personal conversation with Dr. Robert Redfield, AIDS expert). Condoms do offer some protection against a few STDs; they provide some protection against five out of the twenty-five major STDs. The best risk reduction is with HIV. Researchers estimate that condoms reduce the transmission of HIV by 85–87 percent. For gonorrhea and chlamydia, the risk of transmission is reduced by 50 percent.[89] These numbers may seem impressive, but think about the magnitude of the gamble that safe sex advocates are asking you to take. There is no cure for HIV; the end result of infection is eventually death. With condom use 100 percent of the time, you still have a 15 percent chance of infection if your sexual partner has the disease. Your chances of becoming infected with gonorrhea or chlamydia are more like one-in-two. The long-term effects of these STDs include sterility. Many men and women infected with these two STDs show no symptoms and can unknowingly pass the disease on to sexual partners. Even if you wear a condom 100 percent of the time you can become infected, putting your ability to have children on the line.

While condoms offer only partial protection against HIV, gonorrhea, and chlamydia, they offer zero protection from many other STDs. In fact, for the most part, condoms do not reduce STDs, because most STDs are viruses. They are passed by areas of the body not covered by a condom.

HPV offers a prime example. HPV is the number one STD. Fifty percent of sexually active individuals are now, or previously have been infected with HPV.[90] The chances of encountering an infected partner are very high. Because HPV is a virus, it grows on moist skin and is passed easily.

Safer sex advocates urge young people to have sex with protection. But condoms don't adequately protect you from STDs and the conse-

You can use a condom and still get STDs or get pregnant.

quences can be devastating. Clearly, safe sex through the use of condoms isn't safe at all. In fact, sex isn't even required for transmission of several STDs.

The National Institute of Health (NIH) is one of the world's foremost medical research organizations. The NIH acknowledges that "non-penetrate sexual contact"—or, intimate touching—"is a plausible route of transmission [of HPV and many other viruses] in virgins."[91] Just touching! Why? HPV and other viral STDs are passed by the moisture at the base of the penis and vagina. These are areas that no condom covers. If you want to use a condom and have "safe sex," your condom would have to look more like a full-body wetsuit.

That's why the NIH also said, "HPV transmission was not reduced by condoms."[92] You won't read that on a condom box!

Studies show that if even when their partners wear a condom 100 percent of the time, a woman who has sex with an STD infected man has a 37.8 percent chance of becoming infected.[93] The actual risks may be even higher. One university recently did a study of men and women on campus infected with HPV. Of those who had HPV and had sex without wearing a condom, in just three acts of sex, 44 percent of their partners were infected.[94] If that had been AIDS, condoms would have reduced that number to 4 percent (good news unless you are among the 4 percent infected). Of those who wore condoms, 42 percent were infected, meaning that condoms reduced the risk of infection by only 2 percent.[95] Why the small margin? Because condoms do not cover the area where the virus is spread.

Clearly, safe sex through the use of condoms isn't safe at all.

CONDOMS AND PREGNANCY

Condoms may not fully protect you from STDs, but at least they eliminate the risk of unwanted pregnancy, right? Wrong.

The average woman can get pregnant eight days per month. That equals ninety-six days per year. When the government forced condom companies to calculate their product's failure rate, they found that with an average woman, between twenty and twenty-four years of age, when condoms were used 100 percent of the time, there was a 31 percent failure rate.[96] To put that in human terms, that means that for every ten students who have sex using a condom, three of them will experience condom failure, putting them at risk of becoming pregnant unexpectedly.

Girls can only get pregnant eight days a month, or ninety-six days per year. Only females can get pregnant. But you can get

STDs 365 days per year. Men and women are equally at risk. If a condom has a failure rate with pregnancy of 31 percent in ninety-six days, what is it for an STD in 365 days? Are you starting to feel like you've been duped?

THE CLEAR TRUTH

Did you know that the FDA refuses to certify condoms? Why? Because the failure rate is off the charts. Another government agency, the CDC, says that abstinence is the only surefire way to prevent STDs.[97] The second way is mutual monogamy with a partner known to be uninfected. I call that marriage.

The world teaches that safe sex leads to freedom. The only problem is that safe sex is not safe. Clearly, the difference between safe sex and safer sex is huge. Condoms provide the illusion of safety without significantly reducing the risks. And there isn't a condom or contraceptive on the market that can protect you from the influence of sex on your body, brain, or heart. God desires to provide real safety with His design of no sex outside of marriage. Only His plan for your sex life offers 100 percent protection.

Q 13 A Even though neither of us have symptoms, can we still have an STD?

You'd better believe it! Here are the fast facts about hidden STDs.

• HPV stays totally hidden in the body for ten to twelve years on average; you don't even know you are infected.[98]

- 90 percent of HPV infections show no symptoms.[99]
- With chlamydia, 80 percent of women and 40 percent of men have no symptoms.[100]
- The symptoms for HSV II, also known as genital herpes, are so mild that up to 80 percent have no symptoms or do not recognize their symptoms.[101]
- HIV can incubate for ten to fifteen years with no symptoms.[102]
- Even though these STDs have no symptoms, they can still be passed between sexual partners.

The bottom line is that you can't count on your body to alert you when you or your partner have been infected with an STD. Sexually active teenagers report that pregnancy is their biggest fear, because it's the most visible. But STD infection is a much greater risk. Most of the time there is no way to know if either you or your partner is already infected.

Because most STDs have no physical symptoms, many teenagers believe that they are not at risk. The media compounds the issue by bombarding us with images of sex without consequences. More than two-thirds of TV shows (68 percent) contain sexual content.[103] A recent study found an average of ten incidents of sexual behavior per hour on network TV during prime time.[104] And yet no one on TV seems to be paying a price. When was the last time you saw someone on TV get an STD? People are jumping in and out of bed with each other, and no one ever gets a disease. No one ever asks their potential partners to get tested.

All of this leads to what I call the "credit card approach" to sex. It's the idea that you can play now and pay later. Hear me: You *will* pay. By the time your body starts to show symptoms, the price is already too high.

Girls, imagine making the choice to become sexually active your sophomore year of high school. You never show any symptoms of an STD and you never get tested. Several years later you meet the man of your dreams. You marry and try to start a family, but you can't get pregnant. When you go to the doctor to discuss your infertility, your doctor tells you that you have PID. You have had no symptoms but at one time were infected with chlamydia. You now have to drive home and tell your husband that he will never have children of his own.

Guys, imagine a similar scenario. You lose your virginity to a girl you thought you loved at age fifteen. Ten years later you learn what true love is when you meet and marry your wife. She is a virgin on your wedding day. Several years into your

The media bombards you with images of sex without consequences.

marriage your wife begins to experience abnormal bleeding. She goes to the doctor and discovers she has cervical cancer, likely caused by HPV that you unknowingly gave to her. Even though she chose to wait, she is forced to pay a huge price because you didn't.

By the time you realize you've been infected, your body may already be damaged and you may have unknowingly passed an STD on to someone you care about.

So how can you know if your partner is infected? You can't. It's impossible to completely avoid choosing partners who are infected when they themselves may not know. The only guaranteed way is to have sex with one partner for your entire lifetime and to choose a partner who has only had sex with you. The only guarantee that you're safe from hidden illnesses that show no symptoms is to stick to God's plan.

You cannot count on your body to warn you before sex puts you in danger. But God clearly says, "I love you so much, and I want to protect and provide for you to have the most fulfilling experience in sex. So wait."

14 Can you get a shot or take an antibiotic if you get an STD?

When it comes to treatment of STDs, there are no quick fixes. For nineteen of the twenty-five STDs there is no cure.[105] That means, for more than 75 percent of infections, there is nothing you can do once you've been infected.

The CDC reports that an estimated 65 million Americans have an incurable STD.[106] You cannot disregard God's plan for sex and then quickly dismiss the consequences. Simply acknowledging that STDs are a potential danger isn't enough. One study showed that girls were not influenced even when they knew about STDs.[107] They knew the facts but did not understand the dangers. Let me spell it out clearly for you.

HPV is the most common STD. Six million Americans are infected each year. The end result of infection is often invasive cancer.[108] And yet there is no cure. About 16 percent of Americans between the ages of fourteen and forty-nine are infected with genital herpes (HSV); the end result can be serious infection.[109] And yet there is no cure. In the United States, almost 100,000 Americans are infected with Hepatitis B each year. An estimated 5,000 die each year from the disease and its complications.[110] And yet there is no cure.

It is true that some treatments have been developed to prevent STDs, such as the HPV vaccine. But, as we already discussed in the answer to question 8, the effectiveness of this intervention is limited. The HPV vaccine only works for women, and it's about 30 percent ineffective (the National Cancer Institute acknowledges that about 30 percent of cervical cancers will not be prevented by the vaccine).[111]

When it comes to treatment of STDs, there are no quick fixes.

Other STDs do have treatments, but they are often long and painful. Even among treatable STDS, drug resistance is an increasing concern. In 2006, 13.8 percent of gonorrhea cases were resistant to antibiotic treatment, compared to 9.4 percent in 2005, 6.8 percent in 2004, and 4.1 percent in 2003.[112]

The bottom line is that you cannot engage in illicit sex and expect modern medicine to cancel out any consequences. It simply doesn't work that way. The end results are serious, even deadly. The only way to protect yourself from the damage that STDS can cause is to do what it takes to avoid becoming infected in the first place.

15 Is it difficult to get an STD?

Study after study has revealed that young people are alarmingly naive about the risks of sex outside of marriage, especially their risk of exposure to sexually transmitted diseases.

A quick look at the research makes it painfully clear that STD infection is the norm, not the exception, among sexually active young people. Let's review the facts:

1. The CDC estimates that 19 million new STD infections occur each year, almost half of those cases are among fifteen- to twenty-four-year-olds.[113]
2. Today, more than 70 million Americans are living with some form of an STD.[114]
3. Approximately 25 percent of sexually active teens get an STD every single year.[115]
4. One study reported that by age twenty-five, half of all American youth will have contracted an STD.[116]

Keep in mind that these numbers are based on STD cases that are reported. We know that many, many STD cases are never reported due to embarrassment or lack of symptoms. While these numbers indicate your chances of coming into contact with an infected partner are high, your actual risk is likely much greater.

If you honor God's plan, you can have sex without fear of disease. That's sexual freedom.

If you choose to have sex outside of marriage as a teenager, your risk of infection is at least 25 percent each year.[117] If you had at least a one-in-four chance of being hit by lightning, no one would go outside in a thunderstorm. And yet young people are willing to put their lives on the line even though the odds are high that they will become infected with at least one STD with potentially devastating end results.

A recent study by the Kaiser Family Foundation shows that young people have been duped into thinking they can experiment sexually with little risk of exposure to STDs.[118] This study shines the spotlight on some serious myths. Let's combat each myth with the hard truth.

MYTH #1: STDS CAN ONLY BE SPREAD WHEN SYMPTOMS ARE PRESENT.

The Kaiser study revealed that 25 percent of teenagers said that if they were dating someone who had an STD, they would know it, and 20 percent thought that STDs could only be spread when symptoms are present.[119]

TRUTH: MOST PEOPLE INFECTED WITH AN STD DO NOT KNOW IT.

As many as 87 percent of STD cases show no symptoms.[120] Some sexually transmitted viruses, including HIV, can incubate in the human body for as long as fifteen years with no symptoms.[121]

One strategy of government organizations, as well as Planned Parenthood, is to train young people to ask their partners if they are infected. But the reality is that most of your partners don't even know if there is a sexually transmitted infection in their bodies. Even those who do know might not be honest about their health status. Remember this: "An aroused hormone has no conscience." If you take the time to ask your partner in the heat of the moment if he or she is infected, most people will not tell you because they are already aroused. Safer sex advocates will tell you to "ask someone" as a way to protect yourself. Think that through! Are you willing to put your life in the hands of someone else who may not even realize he or she is putting you at risk?

MYTH #2: STDS ARE ONLY COMMON AMONG THE PROMISCUOUS.

Among those studied, 12 percent said that unless you have sex with a lot of people, STDS are not something you have to worry about.[122]

TRUTH: YOU CAN GET AN STD BY HAVING SEX ONE TIME.

One study found that 75 percent of teenagers who have sex before age eighteen have two or more partners, and 45 percent have four or more partners.[123] The world may not consider having sex with two to four partners promiscuous, and yet the chances of infection with even one partner while in high school gives you a 25 percent chance of infection each year. Researchers estimate that within two years of having sex for the first time, half of these sexually active teenage girls may be infected with at least three common STDs.[124]

MYTH #3: STDS ARE ONLY PASSED THROUGH INTERCOURSE.

TRUTH: MOST STDS CAN BE SPREAD WITHOUT INTERCOURSE BECAUSE THEY ARE VIRUSES.

Nineteen percent of young people ages fifteen to seventeen do not know that STDs can be spread through oral sex.[125] Viruses such as HPV grow on warm moist skin. They can be passed through oral sex and even by sexual touching. Avoiding intercourse while participating in other sexual activities, including oral sex, *won't* protect you.

Ignoring God's boundaries for sex is a scary prospect.

If you want to know if you can have sex outside of marriage and not get infected, the answer is probably no. A better question is, "How can I best protect myself from the dangers of sex?" The answer is to stick to God's plan.

If you consider the data on STDs, you will realize that ignoring God's boundaries for sex is a scary prospect. In contrast, if you honor God's plan, you can have sex without fear of disease. You will never have to worry about antibiotics or condoms or dangerous viruses hiding in your body. That's sexual freedom. It doesn't cost you to wait. The hard truth is, when you choose not to wait, chances are that the cost will be very, very high.

16 Can STDs be linked to serious illnesses like cancer?

A Kaiser Family Foundation Study found that 60 percent of fifteen- to seventeen-year-olds did not know that STDs can cause some kinds of cancer.[126] The truth is that STDs are linked to many serious illnesses, including cancer. Understanding this simple truth could save your life.

The clearest example that STDs can lead to serious illnesses is HPV. Researchers have documented a clear link between HPV and cancer. In fact, HPV is the leading cause of cervical cancer.[127]

The UCLA Medical Center observed that up to 99 percent of cervical cancer patients had contracted HPV.[128] Worldwide, approximately 70 percent of cervical cancers are due to HPV.[129] One Johns Hopkins study revealed that 80 percent of sexually active women can expect to get an HPV infection at some point in their lives.[130] As a result, an estimated 500,000 women are diagnosed with cervical cancer around the globe each year. Approximately 300,000 of those women die from their disease.[131]

Cervical cancer is not the only risk. The CDC reports that HPV caused 25,000 cases of cancer in the U.S. between 1998 and 2003, including cervical cancer, anal cancer, and mouth cancer.[132]

You are not invincible. If you play around sexually, STD infection can happen to you.

According to an article published in the *Journal of Infectious Diseases,* anal infections of HPV appear to be as common as cervical infections. As a result, more than 4,600 people are diagnosed with anal cancer in the U.S. each year. Approximately 700 patients die from their disease.[133]

An individual with an HPV infection is thirty-two times more likely to develop throat cancer.[134]

STDs are linked to many serious illnesses, including cancer.
■ ■ ■ ■ ■ ■ ■ ■ ■

If you step outside of God's boundaries for sex, your odds of contracting an STD, including HPV, are very high. The end result of infection can be a serious disease including cancer. Every year, thousands of patients die as a result of this harsh reality.

Let me remind you that you are not invincible. If you play around sexually, STD infection can happen to you, with the end result of a cancer that could cause your death.

17 Isn't it safe sex if I'm on the pill?

Oral birth control, also known as "the pill," burst onto the cultural landscape in the 1960s. It became a symbol of the sexual revolution that called for "free love" and an end to restrictions on sexual behavior. More than fifty years later, we've learned that sex isn't free. The tiny pill that started it all has done little to protect millions of women from the fallout of their sexual choices.

The pill does not protect you against sexually transmitted diseases. The pill does nothing to cover the areas of your body where STDs are passed. There are twenty-five common STDs,[135] affecting 19 million Americans each year,[136] and the pill does absolutely nothing to protect you from infection. That doesn't sound like safe sex to me.

What about pregnancy? Even the pharmaceutical companies that manufacture the birth control pill admit that it's not 100 percent effective. It is possible to get pregnant even when the pill is taken as directed 100 percent of the time. In fact, the pill has to be taken at the same time every single day to be effective. If you miss a day or even miss taking the pill by several hours, your hormone levels will change and it is possible to ovulate or

The pill does not protect you against sexually transmitted diseases.

release an egg that can be fertilized. Young women are more likely to become pregnant because their reproductive organs are very healthy. One study revealed a 13 percent failure rate of the pill for girls in their teens.[137] In human terms, that means at least thirteen out of every one hundred girls who are having sex on the pill will become pregnant unexpectedly. While the pill does offer some protection against unplanned pregnancy, it is not a guarantee.

The bottom line is that no pill can protect you from:

- a single STD,
- a broken heart,
- the mental changes to your brain that result from promiscuous sex,
- the guilt and shame that often accompany premarital sex.

Kelly knows this all too well. She wanted to wait until marriage to have sex, but when she and her boyfriend, Tyler, started to get serious, she made an appointment with her doctor to talk about her options. Her doctor suggested she go on the pill, and Kelly agreed, "just in case." Kelly and Tyler did start having sex. Kelly was relieved that she didn't have to worry about pregnancy or disease. She believed they were practicing "safe sex." Three months later Kelly tested positive for an STD. She felt angry, embarrassed, and ashamed. A few months later she and Tyler broke up. She thought she had done everything possible to protect herself; but the pill had not protected her from an STD, and it did nothing to protect her from the pain she felt when the intense bond sex created with Tyler

The only truly safe sex is between two people committed to monogamous sex for a lifetime.

was broken. More than a year later, Kelly wonders when her heart will heal.

Condoms can't protect you from the many consequences of illicit sex. Neither can the pill. The only truly safe sex is between two people committed to monogamous sex for a lifetime.

18 How can I avoid getting an STD?

There is only one way to guarantee your protection against STDs—to abstain from sex until marriage. Secular and Christian sources agree on this point: Abstinence before marriage and faithfulness during marriage are the only way to guarantee you will not be infected with an STD. The catch is that if even one partner, either the man or the woman, is not monogamous or has been with other partners in the past, you are no longer protected.

The CDC reports that monogamy is the most effective STD prevention method.[138] A report issued by Planned Parenthood said, "Abstinence and lifelong monogamy will continue to be the most effective ways to avoid HPV infection entirely."[139] Federal guidelines for abstinence education mandate that students are taught that abstinence is the only guaranteed way to avoid out-of-wedlock pregnancy and STDs.[140]

Let's look at what God teaches us in His Word.

Within marriage you are free to enjoy sex for a lifetime without fear of disease.

■ ■ ■ ■ ■ ■ ■ ■ ■ ■

Remember Proverbs 5:18–19? "Let your wife be a fountain of blessing for you. Rejoice in the wife of your youth. She is a loving deer, a graceful doe. Let her breasts satisfy you always. May you always be captivated by her love" (NLT).

The man being addressed in this verse is free to fully enjoy the benefits of sex. He doesn't have any reservations. He is satisfied and "captivated," not anxious or worried about the risks. Who is his partner? His wife, not some girl he met at a party or a girlfriend whose other sexual experiences are unknown to him. He is 100 percent protected from the risk of disease or out-of-wedlock pregnancy because his only sexual partner is his wife.

First Corinthians 6:13 (ESV) warns us that "the body is not meant for sexual immorality." When you step outside the protective boundaries that God established in marriage and have sex with more than one partner, your body is functioning outside of its original design and the risks are sky-high.

IMAGINE THESE TWO SCENARIOS.

1. Ashley and Aaron had been dating for three months. On prom night, Aaron convinced Ashley to have sex in the back of the limo he rented. Afterward, Ashley felt so guilty she broke up with Aaron. Several months later Ashley begins having pain in her abdomen and her periods become irregular. She called Aaron to see if he'd been tested for STDs. He confessed that he had four other partners before Ashley and refused to go get tested. Ashley is too embarrassed to talk to her mom about her

symptoms, and she's worried someone will find out if she goes to the school nurse for an STD test. Ashley had sex one time, and now she worries constantly that she's been exposed to a disease that has no cure.

2. Jacqueline and Mark fell in love their senior year of high school. While they both wanted to be as close to each other as possible, they committed to wait for sexual activity until they were married. Neither of them had ever had a single sexual partner. On their wedding night they had sex without any fear of infection. They are now free to have sex with each other as often as they want with no fear that they will ever get an STD.

Monogamy is the most effective STD prevention method.

God doesn't ask you to abstain from sex until marriage to restrict you or to take the fun out of life. Within the context of marriage, you are free to enjoy sex for a lifetime without fear of disease. The only way to protect yourself against STDs is to understand and live by God's plan for your sexuality.

19 Is there a relationship between premarital sex and mental health?

When it comes to sex, God asks us to wait. He is motivated by a desire to protect and provide for us. Yes, waiting protects us from physical consequences including STDs and unwanted pregnancies. Waiting also protects our brains from the neurological changes that happen when we have sex with more than one partner. But does waiting also preserve our mental health? You bet!

It is an alarming fact that sexually active teenage girls are 300 percent more likely to attempt suicide than their virgin peers.[141] Sexually active teenage boys are more than twice as likely as sexually active girls to be suicidal. In fact, sexually active teenage boys are 700 percent more likely to attempt suicide than peers who are waiting.[142] More than 25 percent of sexually active girls ages fourteen to seventeen said they felt depressed a lot or all of the time in the past week, compared with only 7.7 percent of virgins. More than 14 percent of sexually active girls had attempted suicide in the previous year, compared with 5.1 percent of their nonactive peers.[143]

Everyone is talking about teens and STDs, but no one mentions the devastating toll premarital sex has on mental health. Sexually active teens are three times more likely than the sexually inactive to become depressed and attempt suicide.[144]

Dr. Freda McKissic Bush of the Medical Institute for Sexual Health noted, "One of the greatest risk factors for depression, loss of self-esteem, and a lot of emotional consequences has to do with the number of people you have [sexual] relations with." She went on to say, "The more people you have [sexual] relations with, the more likely you are to have difficulty forming healthy relationships in the future when you are ready to be with one person."[145]

Contemporary culture teaches that sex leads to feelings of happiness, wholeness, and intimacy in romantic relationships, but the reality is much less satisfying.

The American College of Health Association recently released a study that showed that 43 percent of all university students in America feel so depressed they found it hard to function, and 61 percent of students experienced times in the past year when they felt everything was hopeless.[146] This connection between early sexual activity and feelings of hopelessness and depression is not a coincidence.

The problem can become compounded when an individual seeks treatment for feelings of depression. A major side effect of antidepressants is sexual dysfunction.[147] Individuals become depressed as a result of sexual activity and then lose their ability to experience normal sexual function as a result of the medication they are taking for depression.

Sexually active teens are three times more likely than the sexually inactive to become depressed and attempt suicide.

Depression isn't the only mental side effect of illicit sex. A Columbia University study found that sexually active teens are more likely to use drugs.[148] Sexually active young people also frequently experience guilt and shame as a result of their choices. Nearly two-thirds of teens who have had sex say they wish they had waited.[149] The guilt of giving something away that can never be recovered may last longer than any other consequence.

One of the most devastating emotional consequences of sex outside of marriage is a broken heart. Because of the neurochemical response your brain has to sex, it is easy to mistake sex for love. Because of the release of oxytocin, sex bonds you to your partner. Sex always forms an emotional tie. When that bond is broken, it can hurt tremendously.

Sex inside of marriage equals security. Sex outside of marriage leads to insecurity, guilt, shame, depression, hopelessness, and grief.

There is also a spiritual price tag to be paid for ignoring the boundaries God places on sex. Hebrews 13:4 says, "Let marriage be held in honor among all, and let the marriage bed be undefiled, for God will judge the sexually immoral and adulterous" (ESV).

Simply put, sex outside of marriage is sin and sin always separates us from God. Ignoring God's boundaries will result in the inability to be fruitful in the kingdom of God, blocked blessings, and a diminished witness.

God knows that the sexual choices we make affect our emotions and ultimately our overall well-being. That's why Proverbs 4:23 warns, "Above all else, guard your heart, for everything you do flows from it."

20 Is it okay to have anal sex?

Anal sex is sex. God asks us to flee from sexual immorality (1 Corinthians 6:18), and this includes anal sex.

The truth is that anal sex is much more risky behavior than vaginal sex. While pregnancy is not possible as a result of anal sex, STD infection is. In fact, anal infections of HPV appear to be as common as cervical infections. In the answer to question 11, I told you that a woman's cervical lining is covered with columnar cells. Columnar cells are extremely receptive to disease. When a woman reaches her midtwenties her cervix starts to harden and the columnar cells in her cervix are replaced by squamous epithelium cells, which are much less receptive to STDs. Your mouth and your anus are also covered in columnar cells. However, they never change over to squamous epithelium cells. These areas of your body will always be highly susceptible to sexually transmitted disease.[150] Young people who experiment with this risky alternative to intercourse are finding that it can be tremendously devastating because it involves parts of their bodies that are highly vulnerable to disease.

Just as HPV can lead to cervical cancer when transmitted vaginally, it can lead to anal cancer when transmitted through anal sex. The grim reality is that more than 4,600 people are diagnosed with anal cancer in the U.S. each year, and nearly 700 die from the disease.[151] Scientists note that the incidence of anal cancer has been increasing in recent years.[152] Not surprisingly, so has participation in anal sex.

Though oral and anal sex were once considered taboo, teenagers are turning to them in order to maintain their technical virginity. But they are paying a significant price.

Sexual activity always has an emotional component. When your body is aroused, chemicals including oxytocin, vasopressin, and dopamine begin flowing in your brain, bonding you to your partner even when vaginal intercourse is taken off the table. By opting to have oral or anal sex, you are setting yourself up to experience the emotional and spiritual side effects discussed under question 19.

God asks you to save every part of your sexual experience.

The bottom line is that anal sex is sex. It has the same consequences as sex. It creates the same attachments as sex. While it may be increasingly en vogue, it clearly isn't the "safe" alternative many believe it to be.

Regardless of the health risks and emotional pitfalls of anal sex, it is most important to note that it does not line up with God's standards.

Three times in Song of Solomon we are warned not to arouse

or awaken love prematurely (2:7; 3:5; 8:4). Anal sex causes arousal just as much as vaginal intercourse. Those feelings were not intended to be experienced outside of marriage. In Matthew 5:28 Jesus equates lustful thoughts with committing the sin of adultery. You will not be able to engage in anal sex without having lustful thoughts. The physical and mental reaction is the same as if you were having intercourse.

God's standard is not for you to engage in sexual activity without technically compromising your virginity. God asks you to save every part of your sexual experience to protect you from an emotional and physical toll that can be devastating.

21 Is oral sex really sex?

A 2003 series of national surveys conducted for the Kaiser Family Foundation and *Seventeen* magazine revealed that half of teens ages fifteen to seventeen do not believe oral sex is sex.[153] Almost 60 percent of college students do not define oral sex as sex.[154] Perhaps that's why slightly more than half of American teenagers ages fifteen to nineteen have engaged in oral sex and why that number increases to 70 percent when only eighteen- and nineteen-year-olds are surveyed.[155]

Oral sex has become a major social norm, with 50–70 percent of young people engaging in oral sex.[156] Part of the appeal seems to be the common sentiment that oral sex isn't really sex. In fact, some students even report engaging in oral sex as a method to retain their purity. They see oral sex as a way of preserving virginity while gaining intimacy and sexual pleasure. But is someone who engages in oral sex really sexually pure? More directly, is oral sex really sex? A simple vocabulary lesson provides the answer.

The dictionary defines "sex" as "sexually motivated phenomena or behavior."[157] The massive trend of young people engaging in oral sex certainly qualifies as a phenomenon. How do we determine if the behavior is sexually motivated? Ask yourself: Does it result in the arousal, stimulation, and gratification of sexual organs? The answer is absolutely yes.

Your body thinks it's sex. Your brain thinks it's sex. Your heart thinks it's sex. Oral sex is sex.

The bottom line is that your body reacts the same way during oral sex as it does during intercourse. Your hormones are aroused. Your sexual organs respond. Your brain is washed in neurochemicals that work like human superglue to bond you to your partner. You receive a blast of dopamine that makes you crave more of the same behavior. Your body thinks it's sex. Your brain thinks it's sex. Your heart thinks it's sex. Oral sex is sex.

Clearly, vaginal penetration is not the only way to have sex. In fact, there are four situations I would qualify as sex. They are:

1. oral-genital (oral sex)
2. manual-genital (sexual touching)
3. genital-genital
4. penetration

All four situations cause a physical and chemical reaction in your body. All four situations create a bond between you and your partner. All four situations put you at risk of infection from sexually transmitted disease. If you engage in any of these activities, you are sexually active.

22 Can I have oral sex and still keep my virginity?

One-fourth of sexually active adolescents report engaging in oral sex as a strategy to avoid intercourse.[158] Students report that oral sex gives them the intimacy of sexual pleasure without costing them their virginity. But is someone who gives or receives oral sex really still a virgin?

Remember from the answer to question 21 that sex is behavior that is sexually motivated and produces a sexual response. Oral sex affects your body, brain, and relationships just like intercourse. Oral sex is sex.

If you engage in oral sex are you still a virgin? Physically, yes, but that's just a technicality. Remember that God doesn't ask you to retain only your technical virginity. He asks you to "keep your marriage bed pure."

Hebrews 13:4 says, "Marriage should be honored by all, and the marriage bed kept pure." The answer to question 7 determined that purity is best defined here as "containing no foreign element." Any time you are in a highly emotional and sensory situation, including during oral sex, your brain releases norepinephrine and paper-clips the memory of that event to

> **Oral sex affects your body, brain, and relationships just like intercourse.**

your brain.[159] You *will* bring the memory of oral sex encounters to your marriage bed, preventing it from being pure and honored as God commands.

In an interview for this project, a young youth worker related, "My wife came home from a women's group where they would just talk about their lives every week. The topic of sexuality came up, and she told me, 'You wouldn't believe that these women who are now married, happily married, had been involved in oral sex before their marriage and now some of them were actually in counseling because of it; because the memories, the images locked in their minds, are profoundly affecting them now.'"

God asks you to keep your marriage bed free from the memories and consequences that come with all sexual experiences.

■ ■ ■ ■ ■ ■ ■ ■ ■ ■

Choosing to engage in oral sex as an alternative to intercourse won't keep the memories of those sexual encounters from being paper-clipped to your brain. As we will learn in the answer to the next question, it won't protect you from devastating diseases either.

God doesn't want you to be sexually active while technically preserving your virginity. He asks you to keep your marriage bed free from the memories and consequences that come with all sexual experiences.

Ephesians 5:3 says, "But among you there must not be even a hint of sexual immorality, or of any kind of impurity . . . because these are improper for God's holy people." God doesn't give you permission to engage in *some* sexual activities while avoiding others. He asks you to save the whole shooting match for your wedding night and beyond. His motivation is to protect you and to provide the opportunity for maximum sex and intimacy.

23 Isn't oral sex safer?

Millions of teenagers are choosing to engage in oral sex in order to enjoy the thrill of sex while believing they are skirting the dangers of promiscuity. This is a painful and possibly fatal error of logic.

Recent studies reveal that young people don't consider oral sex to be "real" sex, nor do they fear the same negative consequences from their promiscuity.[160] It is true that you can't get pregnant from giving or receiving oral sex, but that hardly makes oral sex a "safe" alternative to intercourse.

In clinical studies oral sex has been associated with gonorrhea, syphilis, herpes, and HPV.[161] In fact, if you have oral sex with five people, your chances of getting an STD are increased 250 percent.[162] Specifically, oral sex puts you on a collision course with infection of the number one sexually transmitted disease, HPV. *The New England Journal of Medicine* reports that your risk of HPV infection is nine times higher for people who have had oral sex with more than six partners.[163] Why does that matter? Because an oral HPV infection makes you 3,200 percent more likely to have oral cancer.[164] Researchers have discovered a direct correlation between the popularity and acceptance of oral sex and incidents of oral cancer around the globe.[165]

HPV was discovered in less than 25 percent of oral cancers in the 1970s. In 1990, 57 percent of oral cancer patients had HPV. In 2000, that number jumped to 68 percent. By 2007, HPV was linked to 73 percent of oral cancers in the U.S.[166]

The harsh reality is that oral sex puts you at risk of infection from serious diseases. Engaging in oral sex also has significant psychological and spiritual fallout. Oral sex will bond you to your partner. When that relationship is over, you will be left with the pain that results with being connected to someone you are not in a relationship with. Many young girls report that oral sex makes them feel exploited and that they are motivated to perform oral sex out of a desire to be popular and "make boys happy."

You can't get pregnant from giving or receiving oral sex, but that hardly makes oral sex a "safe" alternative.

When the popularity or happiness doesn't follow, they are left with feelings of guilt, shame, embarrassment, and anger.

It is true that you can't get pregnant from oral sex, but that hardly makes it safe. You can still get an STD. You can still get cancer. You can still get hurt.

The debilitating and potentially fatal reality of the consequences of oral sex far outweigh any momentary pleasure you may receive. I want you to understand the cost and make the choice not to put yourself in harm's way.

24 Isn't sex a private act between two individuals?

What happens behind closed doors doesn't stay behind closed doors. Sex is not a private act. There is a cost to the individual who participates in sex. There is a cost to the people connected to those individuals, and ultimately, there is a cost to society as a whole.

According to many, sex is a private act between two people. We are told that anything that happens behind closed doors is nobody else's business, that the government has no right to enact laws that affect our private sexual conduct, that schools should not be allowed to teach principles to guide sexual behavior, and that the church should stay mum on the subject of sex altogether. After all, it's the individual who must suffer the consequences, right?

Wrong!

If sex is a private act, why does the government pay large sums of money each year for abortions?

If sex is a private act, why has the U.S. government directed billions of dollars toward AIDS research?

If the consequences of sex are limited to the individual, why does the CDC spend so much time, at taxpayer expense, on STD treatment and prevention?

Because sex is not a private act between two individuals.

Wide acceptance of sex outside of God's parameters has a high cost to society.

Did you know that each pregnant teenager in America costs taxpayers a minimum of $100,000, and there are as many as one million teenage girls who become pregnant every single year?[167]

There is only one way to keep sex truly private: mutual monogamy after marriage.

When unmarried teens deliver their babies in public health facilities, the cost is passed on to the taxpayer. When adolescent mothers go on welfare to pay for the needs of their dependent children, the cost is passed on to the taxpayer. When the abandoned, neglected, or abused children of teen moms must be cared for by a government agency, the cost is passed on to the taxpayer.

Americans are literally paying a huge price for the "private act" of sex. The consequences don't stay behind closed doors and aren't limited to the individuals who choose to engage in sexual activity. There is a cost to our society. There is a cost to our institutions, and there is a cost to the half a million children born to teen mothers each year.[168]

You might say, "I'm not interested in the politics or public policy of sex." Then maybe you will be interested in the number of people your partner is bringing to bed.

The reality is that every time you have sex, you aren't just having sex with that one person. You are having sex with every person your partner has ever had sex with, and every partner those partners have had sex with in their entire life. The memories of those encounters will be, as I said before, paper-clipped to your mind. The diseases you may unknowingly carry will be passed from one partner to the next and to the next. On your wedding night, all the people you've ever had sex with and their partners, and their partners, and their partners will come into that wedding bed.

Wide acceptance of sex outside of God's parameters has a high cost to society.

I once came across a pamphlet that asked the question, "How many of the 64 people you had sex with last night did you know well?" The point is that one act of sex can be traced to scores of people. Sex is no longer a private act when one or both partners contract an STD (which is passed on to others in subsequent "private acts").

Dr. Edward Wiesmeier, director of the UCLA Student Health Center, warns students that, "one chance encounter can infect a person with as many as five different diseases."[169] Psychiatrist Dr. Lawrence Laycob says, "When you are casual about sex, chances are that the person you are casual with has been casual with someone else. So there's a third, fourth, or twenty-fifth party out there that you have no knowledge of."[170] Former Surgeon General

Everett Koop called me and encouraged me to be more forceful when speaking about the realities of sexual promiscuity with teenagers. He said, "You need to warn them that it is a very frightening thing. Today, if you have sexual intercourse with a woman, you are not only having sexual intercourse with her, but with every person that woman might have had intercourse with for the last ten years, and all of the people they had intercourse with."[171]

Sex is not a private act. It doesn't stay behind closed doors.

There is only one way to keep sex truly private: mutual monogamy after marriage. God's plan for sex is for a monogamous man to enter into a monogamous relationship with a monogamous woman in marriage. Under these circumstances no other partners are brought along into the marriage relationship, no diseases hidden in the body are passed from one partner to the next, and there is no fear of pregnancy out of wedlock. It is the only sure way to eliminate the high cost of casual sex. Only in the context of a marriage commitment can sex between two individuals even come close to being considered a "private act."

25 Isn't it better if we live together first?

In the 1950s nine out of ten women married without first living with their partners. By the 1990s one-third of couples cohabited before saying "I do." Today more than half of all marriages are preceded by cohabitation.[172] Since 1980, the number of cohabiting couples has increased by 1,000 percent.[173] But just because it's socially acceptable, that doesn't mean cohabitation is best—as the data clearly shows.

Cohabitation rarely leads to "happily ever after." Forty percent of people who cohabit break up before marriage.[174] Of those who make it to the altar, cohabiting couples are almost twice as likely to divorce as those couples who don't live together before marriage.[175]

From a human perspective, living together may seem like a good idea. It allows couples to spend lots of time together. It is economically cheaper than maintaining two households. Most couples see it as a "trial run" to determine if their relationship can stand up to the day-in and day-out challenges of life without the total commitment that marriage requires. They reason, "If it doesn't work out, we can simply part ways without the baggage and expense of a messy divorce." But research reflects a different reality.

The culture may teach that marriage is restrictive and that married couples are dissatisfied by the constraints of their "ball and chain." But research shows that married couples are actually much better off than those who cohabit. Here are the facts.

1. Married people have more sex.
- 48 percent of husbands say sex is extremely emotionally satisfying and 50 percent say that sex is physically gratifying.[176]
- 37 percent of cohabiting men say that sex is extremely emotionally satisfying and 39 percent find it physically gratifying.[177]

2. Married men live longer.[178]
- Nonmarried men have higher rates of mortality than married people.
- Being unmarried decreases a man's average life span by ten years.

3. Married people are wealthier.[179]
- In 2009, the average household income for married couples was $58,410.
- For a single man, that figure drops to $31,399.
- For a single woman, that figure drops to $14,843.

4. Marriage is better for the kids.[180]
- 25 percent of women get pregnant during cohabitation, but the children of married couples are usually better off.
- Children of married parents are generally more successful and less likely to drop out of school (13 percent verses 29 percent).
- Children of married parents are more likely to earn a college degree.
- Children of married parents are less likely to be idle in their early twenties.

While the perks of marriage are clear, cohabiting couples report problems on several levels. Cohabiting couples frequently have difficulty with communication. Cohabiting couples also struggle with conflicting expectations. Men often see living together as a step to see if they want to commit, while women see it as a move toward that commitment. Couples choose to cohabit to get a foretaste of what mar-

On your wedding night, be an amateur in sex and a professional at your relationship.

riage will be like, but the very things that make marriage work are absent in that situation. Specifically, the commitment that is unique to marriage is missing. It is that level of commitment that allows couples to weather the trials of life together.

When couples marry, they are saying to each other, "I love you. I will stand with you. I am committed to you."

Cohabiting couples are saying, "I like you. I want to see if I can love you," or " I love you. Let's see if love holds up under the pressure of living together."

Cohabiting couples always have a back door in the back of their minds and almost half of them will exit through that door and abandon the relationship entirely. That lack of commitment doesn't make for great relationships. The level of commitment that helps couples transcend difficult circumstances in marriage simply isn't there.

Because cohabitation doesn't make for great relationships, it also doesn't make for great sex. Couples often choose to live together to make sure that they are sexually compatible. The reality is that the "plumbing" almost always works. The bodies of men and women were made to join together. Couples will be right for each other sexually. The sad reality is that testing the sexual waters before making a lifelong commitment will diffuse the passion that draws couples together in the first place.

Men often see living together as a step to see if they want to commit, while women see it as a move toward that commitment.

An article in *Medical Aspects of Human Sexuality* points out: "Many marry a 'dream' hoping that strong magnetic sexual attraction means [living] happily ever after . . . They then find that good sex does not mean a good relationship, but that a bad relationship may lead to bad sex."[181]

When it comes to sex, the mechanics almost always work. Bad sex isn't a result of too little experience or sexual incompatibility. The problem is relationships. The problem is a lack of character, trust, respect, and commitment.

On your wedding night, experience is the last thing you need.

Sex is at its best when a committed couple experiences it together. You cannot transfer what you've done with someone else to your marriage bed. It doesn't work that way. Everyone who has premarital sex is robbing his or her future spouse of a phenomenal area of growth together as a couple.

Don't let the culture lie to you by telling you that you need to give marriage and all of its benefits a trial run. In order to experience maximum sex and intimacy, make it a goal that on your wedding night you will be an amateur in sex and a professional at your relationship.

26 Isn't premarital sex really great preparation for good sex in marriage?

The prevailing wisdom is that practice makes perfect when it comes to sex. As we learned in the answer to the previous question, "practicing" the ins and outs of a romantic relationship without the solid commitment that marriage provides, doesn't make for greater intimacy, and it doesn't make for better sex. In fact, sex without marriage is proven to have long-term negative consequences.

In an article titled, "Sex without Marriage Often Ruins People's Health and Well-being," physician John R. Diggs Jr. outlined the specific, and often devastating, consequences of unmarried sex, including promiscuity, abortion, unstable family life, displacement of men, and exposure of women and children to high risks.[182]

Clearly, sex outside of marriage is not "practice" without potential pitfalls. Perhaps that's why research proves that married people are having the best sex. An article titled "Aha! Call It the Revenge of the Church Ladies," published in *USA Today* concluded that Christian women (and the men who sleep with them) are among the most sexually satisfied people on the planet.[183]

Writer William R. Mattox Jr. noted that saving sex for marriage pays considerable dividends. Mattox writes, "Several studies show that women who engage in early activity and those who have had multiple sex partners are less apt to express satisfaction with their sex lives than women who entered marriage with little or no sexual baggage."[184]

In other words, men and women who test the waters of sexual compatibility before marriage are the least likely to be sexually fulfilled. Clearly, practice doesn't make perfect. Mattox isn't the only one sounding the horn on the myth that sexual compatibility must be tested before a couple makes it to the altar.

Practice doesn't make perfect.

In an interview for *Seventeen* magazine, sociologist Dr. Nancy Moore Clatworthy was asked this question: "But doesn't living together before marriage help to iron out some of the disagreements that every marriage inevitably must face?"

Pay close attention to Dr. Clatworthy's answer.

We asked questions about finances, household matters, recreation, demonstration of affection, and friends. In every area the couples who had lived together before marriage disagreed more often than the couples who had not. But the finding that surprised me most concerned sex. Couples who had lived together before marriage disagreed about it more often.[185]

You'd assume that this would be resolved in a living together period. Apparently not. Clearly, there is a powerful link between monogamous marriage and sexual satisfaction. Why? *Because sexual enjoyment flourishes in the context of a committed relationship.* Couples who use sex as a tool to gauge compatibility and determine future commitment lack the level of intimacy, commitment, and trust needed to make sex phenomenal.

Sex outside of marriage isn't "practice." It isn't a "good opportunity to measure future sexual compatibility." It is outside of God's plan for sexuality, and the result is baggage—not freedom. Research shows what God already outlined in His

> **Sexual enjoyment flourishes in the context of a committed relationship.**

Word. Sex doesn't get better simply as a result of physical practice; it gets better with deepening levels of intimacy, trust, and commitment. Premarital sex doesn't lead to good sex in marriage. It leads to disappointment, monotony, risk of infection, and weakening of relational bonds. Waiting for sex until marriage, on the other hand, leads to genuine sexual freedom without fear of consequences.

Do you want to have great sex? Then practice patience and commit to wait for sex until marriage.

27 Sex is so beautiful, how can it be wrong?

Yes, sex is beautiful. It is created by a loving God as a gift for us.

James 1:17 says, "Every good and perfect gift is from above, coming down from the Father of the heavenly lights, who does not change like shifting shadows."

God created sex. His intention was to create a beautiful expression of love and intimacy that binds a couple to each other for a lifetime. But not all sex is the same.

Ecclesiastes 3:11 affirms, *"He has made everything beautiful in its time"* (emphasis added).

When does God make things beautiful? In the right timing. Sex outside of marriage can be pleasurable. It can also enhance intimacy between two people just like it does for married couples. But the pleasures of sex outside of marriage rarely last.

When you have sex outside of marriage, the lines between love and lust are blurred.

Hebrews 11:25 calls the pleasures of sin "fleeting" (NLT). The beauty of premarital sex is brief, passing, and short-lived. In reality, young people who have sex outside of God's design can expect to encounter a range of consequences including depression, rejection, anger, insecurity, suicide, STDs, and pregnancy.

Much of the emotional fallout of illicit sex comes from a misunderstanding of love. Couples say, "Sex is beautiful because it is an expression of our love," but remember that the dopamine produced in your brain during sexual activity doesn't know if it's married or not. Oxytocin doesn't know if it's married or not. Vasopressin doesn't know if it's married or not.[186] When you have sex outside of marriage, the lines between love and lust are blurred. It is easy to misinterpret the chemical reactions in your brain for feelings of love. You can't trust your feelings to verify if sex is right or wrong, and feelings of love aren't proof that your relationship is mature or beneficial.

The beauty of sex doesn't mean that sex is always right. Clearly, it is possible to engage in sex in the wrong way at the wrong time. The end result is that sex changes from something that was beautiful and designed for our good to something painful or ugly.

There is plenty of evidence that sex isn't always beautiful. Examples include affairs resulting in broken families, addiction to pornography, rape, child molestation, and child trafficking. These shocking examples prove that sex can be very, very ugly. Just because it feels good doesn't mean sex is right. Just because it seems beautiful at first glance doesn't mean there won't be ugly consequences.

Sex is beautiful—so beautiful it is worth protecting.

A quick look at the results reveals when sex is right or wrong. Sex outside of marriage exposes you to disease; puts you at risk of bearing children out of wedlock; negatively affects your ability to bond; and can lead to depression, insecurity, and increased tendency toward suicide. Mutual monogamy within the context of marriage gives you the freedom to enjoy the pleasures of sex without any of the consequences just listed.

Sex is beautiful. In fact, sex is so beautiful it is worth protecting. It is so beautiful it is worth waiting for.

28 Aren't my hormones too strong? Isn't it unrealistic to wait?

Several years ago, American sex therapist Dr. Ruth Westheimer was speaking to 1,200 students on the campus of the University of Cincinnati. During a question-and-answer session, a male student asked, "Dr. Ruth, what if I can't wait?"

Dr. Ruth replied, "Young man, it's unrealistic to expect you to wait. Your libido is too strong."[187]

Dr. Ruth's assessment is that sex outside of marriage is inevitable. She echoes the message of our culture, which teaches that raging hormones cannot be controlled and that adolescent sex drives are too strong to repress.

Let's think through Dr. Ruth's stance.

Imagine that a young man comes to a sex therapist like Dr. Ruth and says, "Doctor, I really like my girlfriend and I want to have sex with her, but she doesn't want to have sex with me." What would the therapist advise? Probably something like, "You should wait until she is ready." (In other words, "Your libido is not too strong.")

Imagine a different scenario. A young man comes to the sex therapist and says, "Doctor, my hormones are really raging, and I want to have sex with my girlfriend and she wants to have sex with me. What should I do?"

The therapist's advice would echo the advice Dr. Ruth gave at the University of Cincinnati. "Young man, it's unrealistic to expect you to wait. Your libido is too strong."

We *are* human beings; we are not animals. God has given us the ability to make right moral choices and act upon them.

According to Dr. Ruth's philosophy we are only animals, acting from an urge we are unable to control. If that kind of thinking is true, why do we have laws against rape? Isn't it unrealistic to expect a rapist to wait? Isn't his libido too strong? What about a married man? If it is unrealistic to expect a guy to wait before marriage, then isn't it unrealistic to expect him to wait afterward? Do you mean to tell me that young people with a willing partner cannot be *expected* to wait, but an individual whose partner isn't ready can be? Unmarried men can't be expected to wait, but a married man can control himself even when a woman other than his wife seems desirable? Can't you see the contradiction? Is it unrealistic to wait, or isn't it?

The notion that young people can't wait is flawed logic because it ignores one important point. We *are* human beings; we are not animals. As human beings, we are created in the image of God. He has given us the ability to make right moral choices and act upon them.

Yes, your hormones are strong. Yes, it can be difficult to wait, but the bottom line is that sex is a choice. You are not an animal. You are a human being with the God-given ability to love, to think, to create, and to make moral choices.

In an article for *Time* magazine, Lance Morrow wrote, "Teenagers will no more abstain from sex than will the frisking neighborhood dogs, and it is fatuous, punitive, Neanderthal to expect them to; the best that adult authority can do is to distribute condoms to the beasts and hope they will pause long enough to slip one on before their urgencies of crotch propel them into the hedge."[188]

Doesn't it just frustrate you to hear someone talk about you in this way? Wouldn't it feel good to prove that you are not just an animal, unable to control your desires and passions?

In the same article, Morrow admitted that expecting young people to engage in premarital sex doesn't do them any favors. He writes, "The condom-slinger's mentality takes a ruthlessly unennobled view of human nature. The young tend to fulfill expectations. Government-sponsored condom distribution announces that the society officially expects to get copulating dogs."[189]

The culture may expect you to act like an animal. Society may even be encouraging such behavior in some ways. But God's expectation is very different because of His deep love and compassion for each one of us.

Titus 2:11–12 says, "For the grace of God has appeared, bringing salvation for all people, training us to renounce ungodliness and worldly passions, and to live self-controlled, upright, and godly lives in the present age" (ESV).

By God's grace you can say no to the desire to have sex before marriage. Other people have waited. In fact, the CDC released statistics in 2006 that said that 47 percent of graduating seniors are virgins by their own admission.[190] If you've waited, you may feel like you are the only virgin on the planet, but it simply isn't true. There are millions of young people around the world who are choosing to wait to have sex until they are married. Those who have made it to the altar without giving away the gift of their virginity will tell you it was worth it.

Don't give your future away for a few moments of pleasure. Don't let the culture tell you that waiting is unrealistic or impossible. Sex is a choice. Choose to stick to God's design and reap the benefits for a lifetime.

29 I'm not a virgin. Is it too late for me?

I've talked to thousands of young people who mistakenly believe that once they've had sex they cannot stop or turn back. Having already lost their virginity, they see no way to get it back, so they decide it's too late for them and keep making things worse by perpetuating this behavior, going against God's clear and loving plan.

If that describes you, I want you to know that it is absolutely *not* too late for you. It's true that you can never become a physical virgin again. That's water under the bridge. But you can become a spiritual virgin. God *can* wipe the slate clean.

If you've been sexually active, you already know that choosing to have sex before marriage sets your feet on a path with traps at every turn. Emotional trauma, damaged relationships, damaged reputation, damaged self-image, unwanted pregnancies, and sexually transmitted diseases are all there. The path is dangerous, and the longer you stay on it the less likely you are to escape unharmed.

God *can* wipe the slate clean.

This is the hard truth. Choosing to stay on this path simply because you've already had sex is a tragic and foolish gamble. It is not too late to turn and go in a different direction. God has made a way for you to experience His love and forgiveness and to turn away from your past sin and patterns of behavior.

To do so requires you to take specific action.

#1: ACKNOWLEDGE YOUR SIN.

Don't say "I blew it" or "I made a mistake." Don't come up with excuses. Call your sexual activity what it is: sin. This step is called "repentance." Repentance simply means to agree with God that sin is sin with no rationalizations or intent to commit it again.

#2 CONFESS IT.

In 1 John 1:9 we read, "If we confess our sins, he is faithful and just to forgive us our sins and to cleanse us from all unrighteousness" (ESV). Once you've admitted that your sexual activity outside of marriage is sin, confess that sin to God.

#3 ACCEPT CHRIST'S FORGIVENESS.

For many sexually active young people this is the most difficult step. In 1 John 1:9 God promises that He will forgive us of our sin and wipe the slate clean. But young people who continue to have sex outside of marriage often feel cheap, used, and unworthy of God's love, and so they continue to sin. If you've fallen into this kind of thinking, the reality is that you have given up on God's forgiveness. When you refuse to forgive yourself and to approach the throne of God to seek His forgiveness, you are saying that God is a liar and that Christ's sacrifice is not enough. When you consider yourself beyond forgiveness, you are saying that God is not all-powerful and that He is unable to cope with the magnitude of what you've done. Nothing could be further from the truth!

God has made a way for you to experience His love and forgiveness and to turn away from your past.

God's love for you and His forgiveness through Christ's death on the cross is far greater than anything in your past, present, or future. The basis for your forgiveness is not the level of your sin or even your feelings about what you've done. The basis for forgiveness is Christ's sacrifice for you. Understanding this fact is essential.

God in eternity past knew we would sin. So He provided for His Son, Jesus Christ, to take on human flesh and to go to the cross. Jesus had the infinite capacity to take all our sins upon Himself and pay the price. He went to the cross and said, "It is finished," meaning everything that was necessary for you to be forgiven had been done.

Colossians 2:13–14 says, "And you, who were dead in your trespasses and the uncircumcision of your flesh, God made alive together with him, having forgiven us all our trespasses, by canceling the record of debt that stood against us with its legal demands. This he set aside, nailing it to the cross" (ESV).

When you accept Christ's forgiveness for your sexual sin, you agree that God's grace—evident in Christ's death on the cross—is sufficient payment for your sin.

You can make a choice that today is the first day of the rest of your life. You can step off the path of sexual sin and accept Christ's forgiveness. But you can't stop there.

A renewed commitment to God's standards is a choice that often takes determination and hard work.

Matthew 3:8 says, "Produce fruit in keeping with repentance." Fully embracing God's forgiveness for your sexual sin means making choices to keep you from falling back into the same trap. Studies show that if you've been sexually active, you are at risk of going to the same level of sexual involvement in your next relationship. *Bearing the fruit of your repentance means making choices to keep you from returning to sin.* It may mean making the choice not to go to certain movies anymore because they create a battlefield in your mind. It might mean refusing to be alone with your boyfriend or girlfriend again because doing so tempts you to sin. It might mean backing off from romance and waiting a long time before dating again. Just as sex is a choice, a renewed commitment to God's standards is a choice, and one that often takes determination and hard work.

30 Is sexting wrong?

Sexting is a growing trend among teenagers. Research shows that at least 20 percent of all teens in the U.S. have sexted nude or seminude photos of themselves.[191] Most teens see sexting as nothing more than high-tech flirting. They reason, "It's just innocent fun. I'm not hurting anyone."

That simply isn't true. Many young people seem to take the same credit card approach to sexting that they do to other sexual activity: play now, pay later. If you are sending or receiving nude images, you *will* pay a price and you *will* get hurt.

One of the primary consequences of sexting is public humiliation. Studies indicate that a majority of guys who receive a sext will share it with others.[192] You may send an image with the intention that only your boyfriend will see it, but it's not likely to remain for his eyes only. And when the images get out, they're out there forever and the consequences can be devastating.

Sexting reveals the secrets of your body to someone who is not your spouse.

Many teens mistakenly think that sexting is perfectly legal. It isn't. In fact, nationwide, young people are being slapped with serious charges as a result of sext messages that didn't stay private.[193]

In 2007, two thirteen-year-old girls were threatened with charges of child pornography and open lewdness after pictures they took on their cell phone were widely distributed without their permission. When the girls claimed they didn't know what they were doing was a crime, the district attorney in the case said, "Well, as you well know, ignorance of the law is not a defense."[194]

Over the last few years, many teens have been prosecuted as sex offenders for sending and receiving sexual images on their phones. In one case, three students at a Pennsylvania high school sent explicit images of themselves to four male classmates. All seven face felony child pornography charges and a permanent label of "sex offender."[195]

Sexting isn't harmless fun; it is a felony offense. Legally, sexting is creating child pornography. Forwarding it is legally seen as trafficking in child pornography. The young people who are prosecuted for sexting will *never* escape the label they received as a result of their conviction. When they get married they

Many teens mistakenly think that sexting is legal. It isn't.

will never be able to go to school with their child, go to a soccer game, or invite other families over for dinner, because they are sex offenders. For the rest of their lives there will be consequences— all from sexting.

Sexting isn't only illegal; it's devastating. In 2009, a female student from Florida hanged herself after pictures she took on her cell phone were distributed without her permission.[196] That doesn't sound like harmless fun. Clearly, people can get hurt.

These may seem like extreme examples, but they paint an accurate picture of the wake of devastation sexting can leave in the lives of those who participate. Even if the law doesn't catch you, images you send of yourself won't stay private. Those images will exist forever. Your future employer could see them. Your parents could see them. Your future spouse or future children could see them. And then somebody will definitely be hurt.

Psalm 101:3 says, "I will refuse to look at anything vile and vulgar" (NLT). A nude woman or nude man is not vile or vulgar, but God asks us to wait to reveal ourselves in this way until we are married. There is a time and place for full exposure, and it has nothing to do with cell phones or the Internet. God's standards for your love life aren't limited to what happens in the bedroom. Sexting is wrong because it reveals the secrets of your body to someone who is not your spouse.

31 How can I be forgiven and feel forgiven?

Many of you know the painful consequences of sexual sin. You've personally felt the shame, guilt, and loneliness that accompany sex outside of God's timing. The information in this book may have convinced you to change direction and to pursue purity from this point on. You may be wondering if God can forgive you, and perhaps you doubt you will ever feel the relief that forgiveness brings. Please pay close attention here.

The reason you *feel* guilty is because you *are* guilty. Romans 3:23 tells us that all have sinned and fallen short of God's glory. We've already made it clear that any sexual activity, other than that between a husband and wife, is sin. If you've played around sexually, you've sinned, and you probably already know that guilt is an inevitable consequence.

God's Word says that forgiveness is possible and you can walk in freedom even after a prolonged season of sin. You cannot overcome sin on your own; neither can you wipe the slate of your heart clean—but there *is* someone who can.

First John 2:1 says, "My little children, I am writing these things to you so that you may not sin. But if anyone does sin, we have an advocate with the Father, Jesus Christ the righteous" (ESV). Jesus stands before the throne of God advocating on our behalf for forgiveness. It is only through Jesus that we can be forgiven. If you do not yet have a personal relationship with Jesus Christ, the starting point on the road to forgiveness is a personal, life-changing encounter with Jesus.

Remember that Romans 3:23 tells us that all have sinned. That includes each one of us! If you ask Jesus to be your Savior, He will forgive you of all of your sin. How do you take that first step? By praying a prayer like this: *Lord Jesus, I need You. Forgive me and cleanse me. Right this moment I trust You as Savior and Lord. Take over the throne of my life; change me from the inside out. Thank You that I can trust You. In Christ's name, Amen.*

What happens when you admit your sin and your need for Jesus to save you from it? *He forgives you completely.*

In 1 John 1:9 we read, "If we confess our sins, he is faithful and just to forgive us our sins and to cleanse us from all unrighteousness" (ESV).

This verse clearly promises that

You can walk in freedom even after a prolonged season of sin.

God is willing and able to forgive *all* of our sin. It does not say "everything *except* your sexual sin." No! God forgives *all* of your unrighteousness when you bring it to Him.

You may say, "I understand that Jesus has made a way for my sins to be forgiven, but I don't *feel* forgiven for the things I have done." It is at this juncture that you must choose truth. Don't buy the lie that God's forgiveness doesn't apply to you. That is exactly what Satan wants you to believe. If you are in Christ, the truth is: "As far as the east is from the west, so far does he remove our transgressions from us" (Psalm 103:12 ESV).

God doesn't just forgive you of your sexual sin. He has removed your mistakes completely from you. When the psalmist writes that God removes our sins "as far as the east is from the west," he is using the Hebrew expression for infinity. Think about it. There is a North Pole and a South Pole. You can only go north so long before you are going south. You can only go south so long before you are going north. You can measure the distance from south to north. But

You can't wipe the slate of your heart clean, but there *is* someone who can.

there is no east pole. There is no west pole. If you travel east, you will go east for eternity. If you travel west, you will travel west for eternity. You can't measure the distance. That's how far Jesus removes your sins from you. That demonstrates the depth of His forgiveness.

You *can* walk in the freedom of that forgiveness by choosing to believe what God has already written about you. God wants to forgive you. Jesus has already paid the price for your sin by His death on the cross. When you ask Him for forgiveness, He will wipe the slate totally clean.

32 How can I know if a person loves me?

There are two litmus tests I recommend for recognizing genuine love.

First, if you have a loving, intimate relationship with your parents, talk to them about your relationship. Your parents, specifically your dad, will probably be able to recognize a healthy, loving relationship before you do. Loving parents have great insight into what a healthy relationship looks like for their kids.

I realize that not everyone has a loving connection with their parents. I wish that weren't the case. I wish that every child could grow up with a warm and intimate relationship with their parents. What a difference that would make in the issue of teen sex!

If you cannot ask your parents for their advice about your relationships, there is another way—one found in Scripture—to gauge whether or not you are experiencing true love.

One New Testament passage, 1 Corinthians 13, always comes up when Christians start talking about love. That's because this passage provides a template for what true love is. It shows us, in clear terms, what we should be looking for in a loving relationship. Instead of simply relying on feelings to tell us when we've encountered love, this passage gives us a map of what true love looks like and provides a standard by which we can measure our actions and feelings.

Check out verses 4–7:

> Love is patient,
> love is kind
> and is not jealous;
> love does not brag
> and is not arrogant,
> does not act unbecomingly;
> it does not seek its own,
> is not provoked,
> does not take into account a wrong suffered,
> does not rejoice in unrighteousness,
> but rejoices with the truth;

> bears all things,
> believes all things,
> hopes all things,
> endures all things. (NASB)

A practical way to apply this passage if you're in a dating relationship is to substitute your partner's name in place of "love." For example, if Andrea is starting a relationship with Matt, she would substitute his name in this passage like this:

> Matt is patient,
> Matt is kind,
> Matt is not jealous,
> Matt does not brag,
> Matt is not arrogant,
> Matt does not act unbecomingly, etc.

Go back and review the passage with your partner's name in place. How accurate is the description? If you are in a premarital sexual relationship, this list won't fit your partner well because sex outside of God's boundaries is not patient or kind, and it is driven by selfish motives. If, however, your partner does meet the qualities listed in this passage, you are likely in the midst of a genuinely loving and caring relationship.

Loving parents have great insight.

But the secret to true love isn't really about finding the right person at all. It is about *being* the right person. You can't expect a partner, no matter how wonderful he or she is, to contribute everything necessary to create lasting love. How can you know if you are ready to offer true love to someone else? Substitute your own name in the passage above. Are you loving? Are you kind? Or are you jealous and easily provoked? Are your actions and thoughts directed for the benefit of the other? Are you ready to value your partner's happiness and well-being above your own? If not, you need time to grow and to let genuine love develop.

The secret to true love isn't really about finding the right person; it is about *being* the right person.

Let's go back to the definition of love from question 4. God's Word provides the simplest definition of love—to protect and provide. True love always, without exception, seeks the best interest of the loved one. Its motivation is always to protect and provide. How can you know if you are truly loved? Does your partner do everything possible to provide for your well-being and protect your heart? Do you do the same for him or her? If not, take some time to allow God to teach you how to love others well and to wait for true love in His timing.

33 How can I know God's will?

When it comes to romantic relationships, the Bible provides a clear picture of God's will.

In 1 Thessalonians 4:1, Paul writes this to the believers in Thessalonica: "Finally, then, brothers, we ask and urge you in the Lord Jesus, that as you received from us how you ought to walk and to please God, just as you are doing, that you do so more and more" (ESV). He was writing about how to please God. And then Paul encouraged them, "You guys are actually doing it! You are living out God's will more and more."

In verses 2 and 3 he continues: "For you know what instructions we gave you through the Lord Jesus. For this is the will of God, your sanctification: that you abstain from sexual immorality" (ESV).

What is the commandment Paul gives here? To abstain from sexual immorality. Why? "For this is the will of God." This passage doesn't say that *maybe* purity is God's will, or *sometimes* it is God's will, or it *could* be God's plan for you in some circumstances. No! Sexual purity *is* God's will for your life. And why is it God's will? For our sanctification, our purification, our good.

Do you want to please God? Abstain from sexual immorality. Do you want to know His will? Abstain from sexual immorality. He has told us His will so that we may experience His blessings. Through His Word, God has said, "I love you," which means "I want to protect you and I want to provide for you. So wait!"

Beyond your romantic relationships, how can you know God's will for your life? God's will for us is to be filled with His Holy Spirit. Ephesians 5:18 says, "Don't **Sexual purity *is* God's will** be drunk with wine, because that **for your life.** will ruin your life. Instead be filled with the Holy Spirit" (NLT). This verse tells us not to rely on synthetic influences to find satisfaction. Instead we are to allow the Holy Spirit to influence our life in a supernatural way and change us from the inside out. God's will is for you to be Spirit-filled and to live your life under the control of His Spirit.

First John 5:14–15 says, "This is the confidence we have in approaching God: that if we ask anything according to his will, he hears us. And if we know that he hears us—whatever we ask—we know that we have what we asked of him."

What a promise! When we ask God for something that He

intends for us to have, He is going to give it to us! God wants us to be filled with His Spirit. He wants to teach us to be more and more like Him. He wants to give us power in our sexual lives. He wants sex to be a gift we wait to open with our spouse. We can count on Him to stick to His promises and to deliver blessings when we live according to His will. Can He count on you?

34 How can I say no?

You *can* resist the pressure to have sex outside of marriage. You *can* stand against pressure from your peers and from the media and keep your commitment to abstain. Purity is possible—but it won't happen by accident. You need to have strategies in place to keep your feet on the right path. Here are eleven strategies proven to work.[197]

1. HAVE AN ACCOUNTABILITY STRUCTURE.

Choose friends who have the same convictions about sex as you do and spend the bulk of your time with them. Pursuing purity can be a battle. Don't go at it alone. Friends with the same commitment are your best defense.

Ecclesiastes 4:9–10 tells us, "Two are better than one, because they have a good reward for their toil. For if they fall, one will lift up his fellow. But woe to him who is alone when he falls and has not another to lift him up!" (ESV).

Never stop seeking supportive friends. Create a support structure that includes friends, a youth pastor, teachers, and wise adults who are willing to ask the tough questions. Pursue people who can help you set boundaries and will walk with you along the path of purity.

2. SET CLEAR BOUNDARIES *BEFORE* YOU NEED THEM.

Your body wasn't designed to be able to just stop feeling things sexually. It was designed to continue to move toward sex in the context of a committed marriage relationship. If you get into a situation where things get physical or your mind is allowed to dwell on sexual images, it will be hard to pull up the reins. Set clear boundaries about what you will do physically and what situations you will allow yourself to be in, ahead of time, before the opportunity arises.

Purity is possible— but it won't happen by accident.

For example, in order to avoid the temptation to look at pornography you might establish a boundary that you will only look at the computer in a public room when others are around. In order to avoid becoming overly physical with your boyfriend or girlfriend, you might establish the boundary that you will never be alone with your significant other in a parked car, an empty house, or anywhere else you might be tempted to compromise your standards.

3. WRITE IT DOWN.

Write down your commitment to abstain from sex. Take the time to physically write it out so that your heart can be guarded by your mind. Once you are in a romantic relationship, take time to write down the boundaries for your relationship with your partner. There is real power in writing it down and seeing your commitment spelled out in black and white.

4. ASK GOD TO HELP.

You may have chosen the path of purity out of a desire to please God, but have you actually talked to Him about it? Have you gone to Him in prayer and specifically asked Him to help you stay pure? I suggest praying a prayer like this: *Jesus, I need Your help. I cannot do this by myself. I need Your strength to fill me up and help me be sexually pure.*

Paul said, "When I am weak, then I am strong" (2 Corinthians 12:10). God is able to supply the strength you need to persevere. Ask Him for it!

5. DELAY ROMANCE.

Studies have shown a profound link between early dating and early sex. Dating brings a couple together physically and emotionally. Closeness prompts physical contact, which releases powerful bonding hormones and revs up the powerful sexual engines for both parties. Research proves that the younger young people begin to date, the more likely they are to become sexually active.

For example, of those young people who begin dating at age twelve, 91 percent will have sex before graduating from high school. Of those who delay dating until age fifteen, 40 percent loose their virginity in high school. Of those individuals who wait until age sixteen to begin dating, only 20 percent have sex before graduation.[198]

Waiting for romance will help you wait for sex.

6. DON'T GET INVOLVED WITH SOMEONE WHO DOES NOT SHARE YOUR VALUES.

"Do not be unequally yoked with unbelievers. For what partnership has righteousness with lawlessness? Or what fellowship has light with darkness?" (2 Corinthians 6:14 ESV). This passage warns against linking your life with someone who doesn't share your commitment to faith or purity. If your partner isn't a committed Christian and isn't committed to following God's standards for sex, purity will be an uphill climb. As part of your commitment to sexual purity, commit to date only individuals with the same standard.

7. MAKE YOUR VALUES KNOWN.

How will you know if the person you are considering dating shares your values? Ask! Be upfront about your values, specifically your values concerning sex and relationships. If you don't let your values be known up front, it is going to be much more difficult once the relationship has progressed.

8. PLAN AHEAD.

Plan your dates ahead. Be specific about where you are going, what you will do, and who else will be involved. You almost never get into trouble when you plan things out. When you don't have a specific date plan and are left with idle time, the opportunity to compromise becomes a bigger threat.

9. INTRODUCE YOUR DATE TO YOUR PARENTS.

Remember from the answer to question 32 that one of the litmus tests for the health of a relationship is the approval of your parents. Let your parents talk to your date. Consider double-dating with your parents in the early stages of the relationship. Few people know you as well as your parents. Letting them into your love life provides built-in accountability and helps you judge if the person you're dating will help you stay pure. My wife, Dottie, and I double-dated with some of our kids and their dates. To this day, we treasure the memories of those times—and so do our children!

10. AVOID ALCOHOL AND DRUGS.

A recent study showed that 23 percent of high school students used drugs or alcohol during their most recent sexual experience. Even more alarming, a quarter of teens say they've participated in sexual activity, while using drugs or alcohol, that they would have forgone had they been sober.[199] Many teenagers report that they were under the influence of alcohol when they had their first sexual experience.[200]

It is an accepted fact that substance abuse impairs your ability to make logical decisions including sound judgments about sexual behavior. If you want to abstain from sex until marriage and avoid the risks that come with sexual experimentation, steer clear of drugs and alcohol.

11. GUARD YOUR EYES.

God's Word tells us that we are what we think. Proverbs 23:7 says, "For as he thinks within himself, so he is" (NASB).

The bottom line is: what you think about will affect *what* you do and *who* you become. Be mindful that the way sex is portrayed in the media today is falsely alluring. Exposing yourself to phony stimulants including TV, video, movies, and online articles with unrealistic and unholy portrayals of sex *will* affect you. I'm *not* saying, "Don't ever go to the movies, watch TV, or spend time on the Internet." Scripture does not teach us that

Pursuing purity can be a battle. Don't go at it alone.

media itself is sinful. I am saying to be discerning. Guard your mind against anything that could hinder you in your pursuit of purity.

"Finally, brothers, whatever is true, whatever is honorable, whatever is just, whatever is pure, whatever is lovely, whatever is commendable, if there is any excellence, if there is anything worthy of praise, think about these things" (Philippians 4:8 ESV). This is where we need to choose (as an act of our will) to set our minds on things that will not cause us to compromise our values. Only we can make that choice!

35 How far is too far?

Have you ever thought purity would be a lot easier to attain if the Bible clearly said, "Here is exactly how far you can go physically and remain pure"? Does it seem that if God drew a hard line in the sand, it would make it easier for you to know how to behave?

Hard and fast rules may seem like a good idea when it comes to physical activity, but I'm not convinced they would solve our temptation issues. If God drew an exact line dividing acceptable physical contact from the unacceptable, everyone would race right to that line and then push it "just a little bit" farther. It is our human nature to sin and to push back against authority. If the Bible gave us a bunch of rules, many would find a way around those rules. In His wisdom, God didn't just list a bunch of rules for physical behavior before marriage in His Word. He did something better by giving us principles in His Word that we can apply to our relationships.

Consider these principles as checkpoints on the path to purity. If your values and the level of your physical activity in your dating relationship allow you to stick to these principles, you have strong boundaries in place. If, on the other hand, the level of physical contact in your relationship violates even one of these principles, pull back and reevaluate your boundaries.

THE "WHATEVER" PRINCIPLE

Philippians 4:8 says, "Finally, brothers, whatever is true, whatever is honorable, whatever is just, whatever is pure, whatever is lovely, whatever is commendable, if there is any excellence, if there is anything worthy of praise, think about these things" (ESV).

The question you should be asking is *not*, "How far can we go without getting into trouble?" but, "What can we do to think about things that are pure and honorable?"

Can you hold hands and think thoughts that are pure and honorable? Probably. Can you hug and think pure thoughts? Maybe. What about kissing? Making out? Sexual touching? Having oral sex? Clearly there is a point when your actions will cause your thoughts to shift away from what is pure and honorable and true and toward a desire for increased sexual contact. Don't decide where your line is after your thoughts have switched to the impure. Decide ahead of time how far you think you can go and still keep your thoughts fixed on the things of God. This is a great standard to discuss with your parents, your youth pastor, or a trusted adult.

> **Don't ignite a fire of passion in your partner with the way that you behave.**

THE "NO HINTING" PRINCIPLE

Ephesians 5:3 says, "But among you there must not be even a hint of sexual immorality, or of any kind of impurity, or of greed, because these are improper for God's holy people."

God's Word doesn't suggest that we get as close to the line of sexual sin as possible. Quite the opposite: this passage tells us not to even hint at sexual sin.

Are you hinting at sexual sin when you spend hours passionately kissing on your girlfriend's couch? Are you hinting at sexual sin when you hold each other for prolonged periods, leaving each other wanting more and more physical contact? Are you hinting at sexual sin when your rub each other's private areas even outside of clothing? If you are hinting at sex, you're going too far.

THE PRINCIPLE OF THE "UNLIT FIRE"

If purity is your goal, make a commitment never to cause another person to want to go all the way. At all times consider whether your actions might cause your partner to want to become more physically involved. That includes what you see on dates (movies, videos, TV shows), what you do when you're together, how you relate to each other, how you touch . . . everything you do!

If you are hinting at sex, you're going too far.
■ ■ ■ ■ ■ ■ ■ ■ ■ ■

Don't ignite a fire of passion in your partner with the way that you behave. For some people a goodnight kiss would be totally innocent. For others, it lights a fire of passion and a desire to go farther and farther.

All three of these principles have a common theme. Instead of thinking, "How far can I go?", the Bible teaches us to ask, "How much can I save for my future spouse and preserve in order to experience God's best?"

36 What can I say to those pressuring me to compromise?

Here's a list of our favorite comebacks for those who will tell you not to wait. Use them anytime someone tries to lie to you by telling you that sex outside of God's design is worth the risk.

"WELL, EVERYONE IS DOING IT!"

"Then it shouldn't be too hard to find somebody else."

"IF YOU LOVED ME, YOU WOULD!"

"If you really loved me, you wouldn't have asked, because sex outside of marriage neither protects me nor provides for my future."

"WELL, LET ME MAKE A MAN OUT OF YOU!"

"What in the world does sex have to do with being a man? My dog can have sex. It doesn't make it any more of a dog, much less a man."

"YOU DON'T NEED A MARRIAGE CERTIFICATE—IT'S JUST A PIECE OF PAPER."

"If a marriage certificate is just a piece of paper before you get married, it will only be a piece of paper after you get married."

"AWWW, C'MON, YOU DON'T NEED A WEDDING RING—IT'S JUST A PIECE OF METAL!"

"It is not a piece of metal. It is a symbol of faithfulness and loyalty to one person for life. If it doesn't mean that before marriage, it won't mean that after marriage. A ring is so much more than a piece of metal. Besides, if your wedding ring is just a 'piece of metal' before marriage, it will only be a 'piece of metal' after marriage."

Sex doesn't just happen. It's a choice.

"WELL, WE NEED TO SEE IF WE ARE COMPATIBLE!"

"It's not about the plumbing. Physical compatibility is not the issue. It is relational."

"NO ONE WANTS TO MARRY AN INEXPERIENCED GIRL!"

"Well, I guess I would be an exception."

"YOU DON'T KNOW WHAT YOU'RE MISSING!"

"Well, I guess that will make two of us."

"I CAN'T HELP MYSELF!"

"If you can't help yourself now, then you can't help yourself later, so I would never want to marry someone like you."

"IT JUST HAPPENED."

"Sex doesn't just happen. It's a choice."

"SEX PROVES YOU'RE A GROWN-UP."

"No, what proves you are a grown-up is deciding what is right and wrong and sticking to it. It takes a person with character."

"IF YOU DON'T, IT MEANS YOU DON'T LOVE ME."

"Well, you saying that shows that you don't love me. In fact, you don't even respect me."

"BUT SEX IS SO BEAUTIFUL."

"Of course sex is beautiful. If it weren't beautiful before marriage, it wouldn't be beautiful after marriage. In fact, sex is so beautiful it is worth protecting."

37 How does pornography really affect me?

Before we can understand what pornography does, we need to understand what pornography is. The dictionary defines pornography as, "The depiction of erotic behavior (as in pictures or writing) intended to cause sexual excitement."[201] When pornography is mentioned, most people jump to thoughts of X-rated websites or nude magazines, and that certainly is porn, but according to the definition we are also exposed to porn when we watch television shows or movies with heated sex scenes, see images in magazines or on billboards that are designed to generate sexual excitement, or even read books where sex is written about in a way that is enticing.

Exposure to porn is extremely common in our culture. In fact, pornography is a $13.3 billion industry.[202] Studies indicate that 40 million adults regularly visit Internet porn sites. That's more than ten times the number who regularly watch baseball.[203] There are at least 40,000 porn sites on the World Wide Web.[204] More than 60 percent of all website visits are sexual in nature,[205] and sex is the number one searched-for topic on the Internet.[206] Clearly, exposure to porn is widespread.

The face of porn users is changing to include female participants and young people. In fact, 70 percent of eighteen- to twenty-four-year-olds visit a pornographic website in a typical month. The average age of first Internet exposure to porn is age eleven.[207] In addition, the average teenager watches three hours of television a day, mostly during prime time when sexual content is heavy.[208] Women make up 35 percent of porn addicts.[209]

Since you're living in a culture in which pornography is more common than America's favorite pastime, you may be tempted to think that porn is no big deal. You may say, "It's not hurting anybody," or "It's just for fun," or "I'll quit later." In fact, many young people rationalize that they can use porn before marriage and then stop after marriage because they will have the real thing. The reality is that it doesn't work that way.

Remember that under question 7, we explored the ways that sexual experiences affect your brain? Pornography is designed to be sexually stimulating. When you see an explicit scene in a movie or look at sexual images online, your brain has the same neurochemical response it would if you were engaging in sexual contact with an actual partner. Your body releases a heavy dose of the feel-good

chemical dopamine and becomes washed in oxytocin or vasopressin, which work like human superglue to bond you to your
partner, even if that partner is virtual.

God intended for you to be sexually stimulated by your spouse.
When you use pornographic images for sexual stimulation, you
bond with that image. Even though you are not actually having sex
with multiple partners, your brain thinks you are. What's more,
because exposure to porn is highly

Pornography reduces sex to simply a physical act.

sensory, it causes a release of the
memory chemical, norepinephrine,
which paper-clips those images to
your brain. As a result, you cannot avoid bringing the images
you've seen through exposure to porn into your marriage bed. Because of the way your brain responds to porn, exposure to pornography can damage your ability to bond with your spouse.

Because looking at porn provides a heavy dose of dopamine, it
has been proven to be progressive and addictive. When you marry,
you may genuinely want to bond with your spouse, but because of
exposure to porn, you will require more and more stimulating images in order to get the neurochemical response you crave.

Exposure to pornography has been proven to twist the user's
views about sexuality. One study showed that exposure to porn
clearly causes people to believe:

- the greatest sexual joy comes without an enduring commitment.
- partners expect each other to be unfaithful.
- there are health risks in repressing sexual urges.
- children are liabilities and handicaps.[210]

Another study showed that exposure to pornography stimulates
aggressive sexual feelings.[211] Researchers have also noted that teens

exposed to a lot of sexual content on TV (often called soft-core porn) are twice as likely to have sex in the following year than those exposed to little content. That same study also showed an increase in other sexual behaviors including kissing, petting, and oral sex among twelve- to seventeen-year-olds who had frequent exposure to sexual imagery. Researchers concluded that pornography, even when it's soft-core, creates the impression that sex is more central to daily life than it really is and causes young people to seek out sexual experiences.[212]

The bottom line is that exposure to pornography *will* affect you in terms of your attitudes, perceptions, and values about sex, and porn use can lead to increased sexual aggressiveness and experimentation.

The depiction of sex portrayed by porn isn't real, and it doesn't line up with God's design. Specifically, porn promotes sexual promiscuity, marital infidelity, sexual deviancy, and "no-consequences" sex. People who use porn become conditioned to treat others of the opposite sex according to the patterns they've seen by looking at images in a magazine or pixels on a screen, but pornography pro-

Exposure to pornography twists the user's views about sexuality.

vides a script for sexual interaction that doesn't line up with reality.

Perhaps the most devastating impact of pornography is that it reduces sex to simply a physical act. Porn removes the emotional and spiritual component of sex. Remember that God designed sex to create lasting intimacy. You cannot be intimate with an airbrushed image in a magazine. You cannot be intimate with a person on your computer screen.

In a research study, teenagers were asked to select from a list of 20 items the six most important to them. The number one choice (67 percent) was a close, intimate relationship with someone of the opposite sex. In most cases, sex was the last item selected.[213]

When we stick to God's design for sex, the result is deep and lasting intimacy. Pornography is just sex, and "just sex" is clearly the last thing you want.

38 Is masturbation okay?

Pornography's guilty sidekick is masturbation. The two almost always accompany each other. As exposure to porn increases, so does acceptance of self-gratification as a means to satisfy increased sexual desires. This is an issue I am asked to address more and more often. In addition, some influential cultural voices have made statements recently encouraging masturbation as a "healthy" practice for young people. The culture may hold up use of pornography and masturbation as a smart alternative to intercourse, but that doesn't make it a wise choice.

Culture is not the ruler we should use to measure whether a behavior is right or wrong. God's Word is our standard of truth. And because of God's Word, we can conclude that masturbation is not okay for three key reasons: it's hinting, it's grounded in lust, and it's sex without intimacy.

1. MASTURBATION IS "HINTING."

Ephesians 5:3 defines God's standard of purity: "But among you there must not be even a hint of sexual immorality."

Masturbation creates the same physical response as sexual intercourse. Just because it doesn't involve someone else doesn't mean it doesn't hint at sex.

2. MASTURBATION IS GROUNDED IN LUST.

There is no doubt about it; God's standard of purity is high. In fact, Jesus tells us that sexual purity involves more than our outward behavior; it also includes our thought life.

In Matthew 5:28 Jesus said, "But I tell you that anyone who looks at a woman lustfully has already committed adultery with her in his heart." Jesus' standard was enough to cause a stir in His day, and it is still shaking things up in ours. The world will tell you to get as close to the line as possible when it comes to sex, but that does little more than create a battlefield in your mind.

We find more evidence that lust is serious business in Colossians 3:5: "Put to death, therefore, whatever belongs to your earthly nature: sexual immorality, impurity, lust, evil desires and greed, which is idolatry."

> **Sexual purity involves more than our outward behavior; it also includes our thought life.**

Don't dabble in it. Don't experiment with lust. Don't ignite sexual passions hoping there won't be serious repercussions. Put it to death. Run. Flee. Stop.

3. MASTURBATION IS SEX WITHOUT INTIMACY.

Throughout this book we've highlighted the fact that God created sex with a specific design in mind. In Genesis 2 we are given a beautiful picture of the unique bond between men and women when the Scripture describes the man and wife becoming "one flesh." That is the unique power of sex between a husband and wife—it binds them together and makes them "one."

Masturbation doesn't bind you to anyone. It is an activity done alone and usually in secret. Just like exposure to porn, masturbation can be highly addictive. You will require more and more of the same activity in order to get the dopamine blast you want. Once married, you may experience sexual dysfunction because

Shame has no place in God's plan for your sexuality.
■ ■ ■ ■ ■ ■ ■ ■ ■ ■

your body has been trained to respond without the connection of a partner. As a result there is almost always a great deal of shame attached to it.

Shame has no place in God's plan for your sexuality. Sex is designed to be a gift shared between you and your spouse. When sex is shared between a husband and wife who have adhered to God's purity standard, there is no shame. Why experiment with sex under any other circumstances?

39 What can I do if I feel like I cannot stop my pattern of sin?

As I've highlighted throughout this book, sexual stimulation leads to a powerful release of the feel-good chemical dopamine in the brain. Dopamine works very much like a drug. Increased levels of the same activity are needed to get the same "high" that the original sexual encounter produced. As a result, it is possible for sexual activity—including "outercourse" (nonpenetrative sex including heavy petting), masturbation, and looking at porn—to become highly addictive.

If you've experimented in any of these areas, you already know that once you've started down the path of sexual activity, it is easy to keep going. In fact, you may wrongly believe that you can never overcome your sexual sin.

You may be feeling, "I can't help myself." It's true—you can't. You are powerless to overcome sin on your own. But Jesus came to give you victory over the power of sin in your life.

Philippians 4:13 promises, "I can do all this through him who gives me strength." Through Christ you can have the power to say no to sexual sin. Many young people experience chronic defeat in their battle with sexual sin because they are trying to win the victory in their own strength. When they fail time and time again, they give up and decide they can never be free from patterns of sexual sin.

Because of Christ's power within us, freedom is possible.

This is a dangerous lie because what you think will affect how you live. If you believe you cannot be free from patterns of sin, you will not be free. If you believe you cannot overcome your sin, you will remain defeated. Turning away from sin is not easy, but God's Word promises that because of Christ's power within us, freedom is possible.

Romans 6:6–7 promises, "We know that our old self was crucified with him so that the body ruled by sin might be done away with, that we should no longer be slaves to sin—because anyone who has died has been set free from sin." When we submit our lives to Christ, our old nature dies and God makes us a "new creation" (2 Corinthians 5:17). When we die to self, Christ is able to live in us, and He promises us victory over slavery to sin.

Sometimes that freedom is immediate; the temptation to pursue sinful behaviors drops away. Other times deliverance from sin requires some work. If you are willing to do the work to overcome sexual sin in your life, here are several steps to help you find freedom.

1. ACKNOWLEDGE YOUR UNIQUE PLACE IN CREATION.

Our culture teaches that man is no different from animals in that sex is a need we must satisfy. In order to move toward freedom from sexual sin you need to understand that you are not an animal.

You were made in the image of God (Genesis 1:26), and therefore your desire for sex is not like what animals experience. Your greatest need is for an intimate relationship with God. This is an important truth. If you've been looking to sex to satisfy your greatest needs instead of to God, you've likely experienced defeat because you are trying to fill a spiritual need with physical enjoyment. Acknowledge that you are made in the image of God and that a relationship with Him is your deepest need. Then ask Him to satisfy the longings of your heart that you have been trying to fulfill with sex.

2. ADMIT YOUR SIN.

In the answer to question 29, I said that repentance means to agree with God that sin is sin with no rationalizations or intent to commit it again. Admitting that what you've been doing really is sin is a key step in pointing your feet toward freedom.

3. PRESS IN TO THE BODY OF CHRIST.

One of the most powerful tools God has given us to overcome sin is the church. Galatians 6:1 says, "If someone is caught in a sin, you who live by the Spirit should restore that person gently. But watch yourselves, or you also may be tempted."

Part of the job of the body of Christ is to help restore those who are caught in sin. James 5:16 urges us to confess our sin to each other so that we can experience healing. Confiding in a wise fellow believer is a brave and important step in the process of breaking free. Your Christian friends and mentors are able to provide you with the accountability and prayer you need to walk away from sexual sin.

4. AMPUTATE THE SOURCE OF TEMPTATION.

Matthew 18:8 says this: "If your hand or your foot causes you to stumble, cut it off and throw it away. It is better for you to enter life maimed or crippled than to have two hands or two feet and be thrown into eternal fire."

In other words, if something always leads to temptation, amputate! If you are addicted to Internet pornography, get rid of your computer. If you cannot stop having sex with your boyfriend or girlfriend, put the brakes on your relationship. If masturbation is a struggle, establish some safeguards for how much time you spend alone.

Freedom from sin is what motivated Jesus to go to the cross.

Freedom from sin is possible! In fact, freedom from sin is what motivated Jesus to go to the cross. You can choose to tap into His power and find freedom from sexual sin. "It is for freedom that Christ has set us free. Stand firm, then, and do not let yourselves be burdened again by a yoke of slavery" (Galatians 5:1).

TO THE GIRLS, FROM ERIN DAVIS

Sweet girls,

As JOSH AND I WORKED together on this project, I thought of you often. I knew that one day you would have a copy of this book in your hands and a decision weighing heavy on your hearts.

I know that choosing to live sexually pure is not easy in our culture. I fully understand that everywhere you look, you see the message that waiting is outdated and that sex is the secret to the intimacy you crave. I hate that! I hate that the world has lied to you about sex. Even more than that, I hate that so many of you don't see that you are worth waiting for.

If I could get you to grasp only one truth, it would be that you are already deeply loved.

Jeremiah 31:3 says, "The Lord appeared to us in the past, saying: 'I have loved you with an everlasting love; I have drawn you with unfailing kindness.'" In Zechariah 2:8 God calls you the "apple of his eye." Throughout Song of Solomon, He calls you His "beloved." In Psalm 45:11, He claims He is "enthralled by your beauty."

Waiting is worth it, and you are worth waiting for.

God has been wooing you since the dawn of time. Jesus came to earth and died so that you could be with Him for eternity. He has asked for your heart and promised He will never leave you or forsake you.

There is probably plenty of data to back up what I am about to write, but I know it to be true because I am a girl. Girls sin sexually because of a deep desire to experience love. You may be tempted to have sex with your boyfriend because you think it will bring you closer and seal his commitment to you. You may have already given parts of yourself away behind closed doors because you were looking for affirmation that you are adored. Listen to me: The God of the universe has already lavished greater love on you than you can ever experience in a human relationship.

You are worth waiting for because you are the treasured daughter of the King of kings. Sex is worth waiting for because it is at its best in the committed relationship that can only be found in marriage.

Some of you want to wait, but you wrestle with the loneliness of staying pure. Let me assure you that

Girls sin sexually because of a deep desire to experience love.

you are not the only one. I have spoken to thousands of young women just like you who are waiting. What's more, I waited. And I can tell you, from experience, I am so glad I saved every part of my body and my heart for my wedding night. The intimacy I experience with my husband, even after ten years of marriage, far outweighs every moment of loneliness or anxiety I felt while waiting on God's timing.

Waiting is possible. Waiting is worth it, and you, sweet girl, are worth waiting for.

A fan,
Erin

TO THE GUYS, FROM JOSH MCDOWELL

W HAT A THRILL it would be to spend time with each of you, like a father with his son. We would discuss openly the tough issues and would so want you to wait. My love for you would desire you to wait in order to protect you from the devastation that always accompanies sex outside of God's boundaries.

Consider these final words a conversation just between us. This is our chance to talk, man-to-man, about the issues of sex and purity.

Before we go any further, I want you to know why you matter. As men, we all want to know that we have what it takes. We deeply desire the respect and appreciation of those around us.

God's Word is clear that you matter a great deal. He has entrusted you with the mission of living like Him and sharing the message of the gospel with others. Clearly, you have value in the kingdom of God. Your value comes from God—not from any exploits (sexual or otherwise). The world may tell you that you can earn respect by being sexually aggressive or intimate with many women. God says that your value comes from belonging to Him. You don't have to earn your place with Him. He asks you to wait so that you will have what it takes to live the life He has called you to and keep up the fight for the abundant life He has promised.

Purity is proof that you're a real man.
■ ■ ■ ■ ■ ■ ■ ■ ■ ■

It is not an easy task to be called to purity when we are seemingly bombarded from every side by sex. But, here's the thing: Purity is proof that you're a real man. Real men don't just do what other people are doing. Real men make decisions that protect the people they care about. In fact, by choosing to live a life that is sexually pure, a life that honors God with your sexuality, you are already providing for your future wife and kids. Think about that! That's a choice worthy of respect.

This journey toward sexual purity is not always going to be easy—you already know this. Find some trusted voices to give you wise advice. Take on the fight together with some fellow warriors. Hold each other accountable, pick each other up when you make mistakes, and keep on pressing toward God's best for your life.

Your value comes from God.

Don't settle for less than sex at its best! Waiting is possible, waiting is worth it; take the lead!

Best,
Josh

A NOTE TO YOUTH LEADERS

Sex isn't easy to talk about. If you work with young people, you know their hesitation hasn't kept them from hearing plenty about it. The wave of our culture's "anything goes" attitude about sex has left a wake of destruction in the lives of too many young people. If we want them to embrace God's plan for their lives, especially in the areas of intimacy, marriage, and love, we've got to give them the bare facts on the issue of sex.

This book doesn't shy away from tough topics like pornography, masturbation, and sex addiction. The goal wasn't to build in shock value, but to talk about the issues that teenagers are struggling with in real time. In order to help maximize the book's potential to impact young lives, we've included six sections of discussion questions. These questions are best used in peer-led discussion groups where students can talk in a safe and confidential environment about what they've learned.

Thank you for speaking truth to the young people in your sphere of influence.

■ ■ ■ ■ ■ ■ ■ ■ ■ ■

We are not encouraging casual conversations about sex. We know that the topics tackled in this book are delicate. But since God isn't silent on the subject of sex, and neither is the culture, we want to equip you to create opportunities for the young people in your group to explore God's truth on this subject.

Thank you for speaking truth to the young people in your sphere of influence. Thank you for equipping them to stick to God's plan for sex and marriage. As we've shared in this book, when sex is enjoyed within the boundaries of God's design, the results are out of this world. By helping young people see God's vision for sex, you're giving them a gift that will last a lifetime!

DISCUSSION QUESTIONS

SECTION 1: QUESTIONS 1–5

1. If purity means "to live according to God's design," what are some ways you are already pursuing purity? What are some areas where you need to adjust your behavior to better fit into God's design?

2. Finish this sentence: If abstinence is a rule, purity is a _____. How does this distinction change the way you feel about purity?

3. Read Song of Solomon chapter 1. When you read these descriptive and romantic verses, how does it make you feel? (Examples: uncomfortable, curious, excited.) Why do you think this intimate conversation between two lovers is included in God's Word?

4. How would you answer the question, "Is God good?"

5. How does your answer to the question about God's goodness affect your choices? More specifically, how does it impact the decisions about sex and romance?

6. Question 3 outlines three specific purposes for sex: procreation, unity, and recreation. Rank these purposes in order of importance. Explain your answer.

7. If true love always seeks the best interests of the one being loved by protecting and providing for that person, what are the examples of true love in your own life? In other words, who has expressed God's definition of love to you?

8. List three ways you can protect and provide for the best interests of your future spouse.

9. What are three unique ways Jesus demonstrated His love for you?

10. Deuteronomy 10:13 tells us that God's commandments are for our own good. List three of God's commandments found in the New Testament. For each commandment, complete the following sentence:

I know this commandment is for my own good because following it means . . .

SECTION 2: QUESTIONS 6–19

1. Science has proven that the greatest pleasures of sex happen in your brain. In other words, sex is really a mental activity. How does this contrast with what our culture teaches about sex?

2. Why do you think God designed our brains so that we are unable to fully make decisions based on future consequences until our midtwenties?

3. Norepinephrine is a brain chemical that takes highly emotional and sensory experiences and "paper-clips" them to your brain for recall. What is one experience that has been paper-clipped to your brain? Why do you think norepinephrine was released during this experience?

4. What is your reaction to the facts about widespread infection of STDs?

5. Prior to reading the answer to question 9, how much did you know about the most common STD, HPV? How does the information presented in this chapter change how you view STDs in general?

6. How should adults approach the subject of STDs with teenagers in order to help stop the epidemic of STDs among young people?

7. How does it make you feel to know that the "safe sex" message is a lie?

8. Does knowing that condoms and the pill do little or nothing to protect you from STDs motivate you to avoid sexual activity? Why or why not?

9. Reread the two scenarios near the end of the answer to question 13. What would your reaction be if you were in one of the relationships described in these stories? How does imagining the impact of your sexual choices on your future mate and children affect your sexual choices?

10. How would you describe the general attitude toward STDs among your peers? (Examples: concern, apathy, ignorance, humor.)

SECTION 3: QUESTIONS 20–24

1. Why do you think there is a correlation between premarital sex and depression/suicide?

2. Think about sin in your own life (sexual or otherwise). Ultimately, how did that sin make you feel?

3. Finish the following sentences with as many words as you can think of.

    Sex outside of marriages leads to feelings of . . .

    Sex inside of marriage leads to feelings of . . .

4. Based on what you've read, how would you define sex? Other than intercourse, what activities would you include in this definition?

5. Why do you think young people are increasingly willing to accept that sexual activity, including oral sex, is "not really sex"?

6. Think back to the story of the wife who told her husband that her friends were in counseling because of their experiences with oral sex prior to marriage. Based on what you now know about how sex affects the brain, why do you think these women were still dealing with the emotional consequences of engaging in oral sex long after those encounters?

7. Finish this sentence: Culture says that only intercourse is sex, but God's standard is that sex is anything that . . .

8. Specifically, how have you been exposed to the lie that sexual activity is okay as long as you retain your technical virginity? (Examples: friends, certain TV shows, movies, etc.)

9. When you think about your future spouse, what level of sexual intimacy do you hope that person saves for you?

10. What surprises you most about the dangers of oral sex?

SECTION 4: QUESTIONS 25–31

1. In your opinion, who pays the highest price when sexual activity is not saved for marriage?

2. How do you think it would impact society as a whole if God's standard for purity were the norm, and not the exception, in our culture?

3. Under question 26 you were encouraged to be an amateur at sex and an expert in relationships on your wedding night. Being an amateur at sex simply means avoiding sexual experiences until you are married. What does it take to become an expert in relationships?

4. In your opinion, what are the three most important needs to have satisfied in a romantic relationship? Would these needs be better met through cohabitation (living together) or marriage? Explain your answer.

5. Why are monogamous married couples experiencing the best sex?

6. How does it make you feel to know that the culture sees you as an animal that cannot control your sexual urges?

7. According to the answers to questions 25 and 26, what are some of the unique benefits of marriage? Which if these perks are most important to you?

8. What specific Scriptures help you stick to your commitment to save sex for marriage even when your hormones or emotions make waiting difficult?

9. Why do you think many Christian teenagers who give away their virginity in a moment of passion continue down the path of sexual sin?

10. What is your reaction to the stories of teenagers who faced legal prosecution for sexting? Do you think this is the right approach to stop sexting? Why or why not?

SECTION 5: QUESTIONS 32–36

1. Describe a time when you experienced God's forgiveness. Looking back, how did God's forgiveness make you feel?

2. What advice would you give a friend who is struggling to accept God's gift of forgiveness?

3. Why do you think God's promise of total forgiveness, even for our sexual sin, is so difficult to accept?

4. Read 1 Corinthians 13:4-7. Go back and reread it and substitute your name every time the word "love" is used. How well does this describe you? Based on this passage, do you think you love others well?

5. Describe a relationship in which you know you experience genuine love. (It doesn't have to be a romantic relationship.) How do you know that you are loved?

6. When do you feel unsure of God's will for you? Based on what you read under question 34, what specific steps could help you discover God's will in that area?

7. Describe your accountability structure. In other words, who is intentionally helping you keep your commitment to purity?

8. After reading this book, what specific boundaries have you established to help you maintain purity?

9. Delaying romance has been proven to be a powerful tool to help young people stay sexually pure. Keeping that in mind, what do you think is the best age to start dating?

10. What involvement do your parents have in helping you stay sexually pure?

SECTION 6: QUESTIONS 37–39

1. The answer to question 37 defines pornography as "the depiction of erotic behavior (as in pictures or writing) intended to cause sexual excitement." What specific types of media fit into this definition?

2. Have you ever been exposed to porn? Did you recognize what you saw as pornography at the time, or did you see it as something more harmless?

3. Why do you think women and young people are increasingly using porn? What is the allure for those users?

4. Which of the impacts of pornography listed in the answer to question 37 is most shocking to you? Why?

5. Fill in the blanks for the following sentence: Pornography leads to _____ sex, but waiting leads to _____ sex in marriage.

6. Why do you think young people who struggle with masturbation almost always deal with a great deal of shame?

7. Why do you think Jesus equated lust with adultery in Matthew 5:28? What point was He trying to make?

8. How does confessing sin to another person help us heal from the devastation of sin?

9. What sources of temptation do you need to "amputate" in order to keep your commitment to sexual purity?

10. How does it make you feel to know that freedom from sin is possible through Christ?

NOTE INFORMATION

The most up-to-date notes are
available online at www.josh.org.

ACKNOWLEDGMENTS

T O DOTTIE AND MY FAMILY for truly living out love in
relationships.

To Pam, Lakita, Sean, Freda, Elaine, and Christie for lending their expertise and insight of this marvelous theme.

To Sue and Kim for their tireless research and for putting my handwriting into legible print.

To Prolifik Films for their professionalism and creative insight.

To Christ Community for allowing the use of their spectacular "coffee show" for filming.

To Erin, so wonderful to work with and so great at what she does.

THE COFFEE HOUSE CHRONICLES

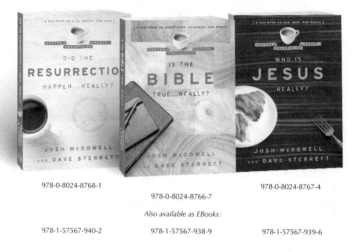

978-0-8024-8768-1

978-0-8024-8766-7

Also available as EBooks:

978-1-57567-940-2   978-1-57567-938-9   978-1-57567-939-6

978-0-8024-8767-4

With over 40 million books sold, bestselling author Josh McDowell is no stranger to creatively presenting biblical truth. Now, partnering with fellow apologist Dave Sterrett, Josh introduces a new series targeted at the intersection of story and truth.

The Coffee House Chronicles are short, easily devoured novellas aimed at answering prevalent spiritual questions. Each book in the series tackles a long-contested question of the faith, and then answers these questions with truth through relationships and dialogue in each story.

MOODY
PUBLISHERS

www.MoodyPublishers.com